WIFE TO THE PROPHET
MOTHER TO A NATION

**DR MUHAMMAD SA'ID
RAMADAN AL-BOUTI**

DHIKR. PUBLICATIONS

Dhikr. Publications
First Published August, 2021
Sydney

Title: A'isha; Wife to the Prophet,
Mother to a Nation: A Short Biography

Author: Dr Muhammad Sa'id
Ramadan Al-Bouti

Translation: Omer Siddique

ISBN Print: 978-0-6450379-2-0
ISBN Ebook: 978-0-6450379-3-7

Other Titles by Dhikr.

The Illumination on Abandoning Self-Direction,
Ibn Ata'illah Al-Sakandari

The Reviver of the Second Millenium: Imam
Al-Rabbani. Shaykh Osman Nuri Topbas

dhikr.com.au

Amr ibn al-As ﷺ at one point questioned the Messenger ﷺ,
'Who is the most beloved of people to you?'
He replied, 'A'isha'.
He asked, 'And from the men?'
He replied, 'Her father'...

- Sahih Bukhari, Book 62, Hadith 14

'For the past few years, it was my routine to prepare food and dedicate its reward to the Prophet ﷺ, Ali, Fatima, Hasan and Husayn. I saw the Prophet ﷺ in my dream, I greeted him, but he turned his back to me (indicating displeasure). The Prophet ﷺ said: "I eat at A'isha's; if anyone wants to send me food, send it there." I understood the cause of his disapproval was that I did not mention A'isha's name in the dedication. Following the dream, I mentioned all the wives of the Prophet ﷺ and his family in my

dedications...'

- Shaykh Ahmed al-Sirhindi.
Endless Grace; Dreams and Visions of the Prophet through the Ages, Dr Muzamil Khan.

CONTENTS

TRANSLATOR'S FOREWORD	6
AUTHOR'S FOREWORD	9
AUTHOR'S INTRODUCTION	14
HER BIRTH, LINEAGE & YOUTH	16
ENGAGEMENT AND MARRIAGE WITH THE MESSENGER	19
A REBUTTAL TO THE FALSEHOOD SPREAD AGAINST THIS MARRIAGE	24
IN THE HOUSE OF PROPHETHOOD	36
A SIDENOTE: THE SACRED MEANING OF THE PROPHET'S LOVE FOR WOMEN	47
THE SLANDER	54
SAYIDAH A'ISHA'S SCHOLARLY PROMINENCE	83
HER SHARE OF ELOQUENCE AND SKILL OF EXPRESSION	91

A'ISHA AND WOMEN	94
THE WORSHIP OF A'ISHA, HER PIETY & ABSTINENCE	98
A WORD ON THE JEALOUSY BETWEEN THE MOTHERS OF THE BELIEVERS	101
DID A'ISHA LEAD AN OPPOSING FACTION?	106
A'ISHA IN THE AGE OF THE RIGHTEOUS CALIPHS	113
THE BATTLE OF AL-JAMAL, A DARK TRIBULATION	125
A'ISHA DURING THE RULE OF MUAWIYA	141
HER LAST DAYS & DEATH	145
HER MOST FAMOUS STUDENTS	148
AFTERWORD	150

TRANSLATOR'S FOREWORD

All praises belong to Allah, Lord of the Worlds ﷻ. May His Peace and Blessings be upon his noble and final Messenger, Muhammad ﷺ. And upon his family, his wives, and companions.

And Praises be to Him ﷻ, that he has allowed this short work from the late Dr Muhammad Saeed Ramadan Al-Buti رحمه الله, the renowned scholar of Syria to be translated into the English language. A somewhat polemic work against those that disparage and defame Sayidah A'isha رضي الله عنها, it is a brief account of her astonishing life and the shaykh's defence of her, her stances, and against those arguments that discredit her.

The shaykh himself mentions that when he was still privately preparing this work, his daughter, and she too did not yet know about it, called him from Riyadh saying, 'I saw a dream. Our door was knocked and when I opened it, a woman entered and said, "I am A'isha, Mother of the Believers and I have come to thank your father."' Indeed, such was the modesty of our mother A'isha رضي الله عنها, that even in the realm of dreams she would not appear before a man she was not related to.

In regard to the contentious issue of her age of marriage with the Messenger ﷺ, of note is that the shaykh doesn't question the classical view that she was 9 when she began living with him. The shaykh notes that in the society of ancient Arabia, it was ordinary for young girls to be married once they had reached the age of puberty. And there are narrations that A'isha was in fact engaged to another man, Jubayr ibn Mutim, before she was engaged to the Prophet ﷺ.

Whatever the reality of her age, to put the customs of today on a society over 1400 years ago is an unfair juxtaposition and is a clear anachronism. Not to mention the fact that there are thousands of authentic reports on the great moral virtues of the Prophet ﷺ. His virtue, chastity, honour, and righteousness is clearly established and becomes the foundation on which all other hadiths are understood. Otherwise, one would just be picking and choosing certain narrations while turning a blind eye to many more that prove the opposite of one's conclusions. It would be like wandering into a rainforest and finding one or two dead trees and then saying - *Nothing grows in this forest, all its trees are dead!* In reality, the entire rainforest is full of life, even the fallen tree trunks he thinks dead.

But we should not let this issue or other controversies from her life, distract us from the great personality that was A'isha, Mother of the Believers, nor from her stellar achievements. As Dr Bouti points out concisely in the following pages, she was a truly unique and remarkable woman. Her huge impact on the Muslim world can not be ignored.

Neither was she a scholar detached from the affairs of her people. Living up to the title of 'Mother of the Believers', she spoke out against any injustice and stood up against any oppression. As it was her right to do so for Allah named her a mother of all believers and isn't a mother worried for her children?

We hope the dear reader, may get a glimpse of the greatness of this noble Lady through this short work, her immeasurable role in the establishment of Islam, and that we all understand once again the crucial role women play in the rise and fall of civilisations.

Translator,
Omer Siddique

AUTHOR'S FOREWORD

All praises belong to Allah ﷻ, the benefactor of every blessing, and may the most bountiful blessings and wholesome greetings be on our master, Muhammad ﷺ and on all his family and companions.

I suppose there are people who follow my writings who might say, whether within themselves or with their tongues – Isn't Sayidah A'isha, Mother of the Believers, deserving of more than just this short treatise about her life and impact on the Muslim world?

Perhaps a driving factor for this question is that a book of this size is strange when compared to my other books, we exclude of course the series *'Abhaath fil Al-qimma'* composed of 10 small booklets. I don't conceal from the reader that I was the first to whom this thought struck. I posed the question to myself before anyone posed it to me.

As for my response I would say that many articles and books, both lengthy and concise, have surfaced on Sayidah A'isha, may Allah be pleased with her, especially in this time. Some looking at her life from a political aspect, others in relation to fiqh (Islamic Law), others academically. Yet others highlight her rhetorical and literary excellence or have concentrated on her life comprehensively, touching on all aspects, sometimes in a literary, flowing style sometimes in a more academic and analytical mode.

There are certain, notable (or controversial) events in her life and stances connected with her methodology, that have given her life an importance far above the cliches and trivialities contained in the lives of others, surpassing those shared, common threads amongst us.

These events and stances didn't pass by the proponents of the various schools of thought hastily and without criticism either. Rather, they stopped to consider them and didn't move on until each shaded them with his own purpose, agenda, and the school of thought to which he belonged to.

And look to the many, different, lengthy publications which have appeared regarding Sayidah A'isha ﷺ, which indicate to us her diverse methods and manner. And suddenly, the notable events and stances from her life become covered – I daresay lost – in the ocean of her sayings, actions and activities, which are presented at great length and sometimes with exaggeration and repetition...The reader can hardly stop at the details of the notable events of her life, yet alone find it easy to study them and visualise them as they are in reality, pure from wavering, personal biases.

My role, in regard to this book, even if only in appearances, is to give a historical account of the life of the Mother of the Believers, A'isha, may Allah be pleased with her. Although in its essence this book is mostly focused on the notable events and stances in the life of this blessed woman ﷺ, I have chosen to shine the spotlight on them with commentary whenever appropriate in the weaving together of the entirety of her life's story from her birth to her death.

Hence, I have shortened the discussion of the general details and expanded as necessary on the notable events and situations.

And so, the book is quite short in respect to being a general biography, yet detailed and extensive in focusing on those important matters and issues from the life of Sayidah A'isha ﷺ.

From the most important of these events that I have extrapolated on are:

1. The Prophet's ﷺ marriage with Sayidah A'isha ﷺ and the confusion some writers have caused by commentating on her youth at that time.

2. The Prophet's ﷺ particular love for her and his regard for women in general as he mentioned about himself in his hadith (his sayings).

3. The incident of the slander, what it constituted of, and its aftermath.

4. The battle of al-Jamal (the Camel), investigation of its real perpetrators and hidden hands involved.

5. Investigation into the different types of enmity against the person of Sayidah A'isha ﷺ.

The purposes of many who wrote about these events was to add their own interpretations and understandings, as dictated by their own agendas and schools of thought they were promoting. May Allah ﷻ forbid that my work too become participant in such biased sacrilege.

My intention is to highlight these events as they were, free from any embellishment that would serve any school of thought or even approach some agenda...my one and only purpose is that we listen to what these events say as introduced by themselves, instead of listening to what they were made to say, as defined by those with agendas who seek promotion for their ideas first and then look for supposed evidence to support those positions, second.

This entails that we, before all else, free ourselves from the chains of pre-conceived notions and from sanctifying hear-say. We praise Allah ﷻ that he has made, through our Islam, the best light to reveal this path, and the best means to be free from such chains.

O Allah, make us steadfast on your guidance and sticking to your commandment: '**And, do not follow that of which you have no (authentic) knowledge.**

Indeed the ear, the eye and the heart – each of them will be questioned.' (Quran; Al-Isra', Verse 36).

AUTHOR'S INTRODUCTION

The study of the life of the Mother of the believers, Sayidah A'isha ﷺ, is not a conventional, historical study. Nor is it purely a religious endeavour. Rather in reality, it is an exploration of complex, interweaving social realities manifested in the life of one individual – Sayidah A'isha ﷺ. For she embodied these social realities as they advanced in the early period of Islam.

After the mission of our master, Muhammad, the Messenger of God ﷺ, she was evidence of the effect of Islam and how it completely reformed the Arabs. These social realities included a new social status for women, now revived under the shade of Islam, a new political effectiveness that allowed the Arabs to compete on the world stage – including the involvement of women in that – as well as establishing the enduring alliance between religion and state. A political state which was mobilised to serve the Islamic vision and protect its fundamentals and laws.

And so, the study of the life of Sayidah A'isha becomes an investigation of a reality that gathers all these different aspects together. Whereas a thorough study would necessarily assume this responsibility to achieve such a goal, a book of this briefness cannot accommodate it or reach its fruits. Rather, such a purpose wouldn't be possible, except in a voluminous work, full of all those various types of studies and investigations.

However, just as encompassing, detailed studies make clear in encyclopedias and volumes their purposes and have their benefits, likewise sound summaries have their own advantages and roles to fulfil. And I have expounded a bit on the purpose of this book in its Foreword.

Perhaps, this brevity of words, of which we are about to encounter, will achieve its desired benefit and aspired-to goal. And I hope it will not be an incomplete summary, but adequate for the purposes of which I had in mind.

HER BIRTH, LINEAGE & YOUTH

Sayidah A'isha was born 7 years before the hijra,[1] according to the preferred opinion. It has been authenticated that she said:

'The Messenger of Allah signed the marriage contract with me when I was six years old and started living with me when I was nine years old.' - The hadith is agreed upon by the two shaykhs.[2]

If we know that the Prophet lived with her in the month of Shawwal after the battle of Badr, in the second year hijri, it becomes clear that she was born 7 years before the hijra. And so, she was from amongst those born in the cradle of Islam, who opened their eyes to its light.

As for her lineage, then her father is the greatest *Siddeeq* (truthful one) to the Messenger of Allah, Abu Bakr. His real name being Abdullah ibn Abu Quhafah. The real name of Abu Quhafah was Uthman ibn Amir ibn Amr, ibn K'ab ibn Sa'ad ibn Tayyim ibn Murra...and it is here that his lineage meets with the lineage of the Messenger of Allah.

Abu Bakr's name during the Age of Ignorance (*Jahiliyya* i.e., before Islam) was Abdul Ka'bah (Slave of the Ka'bah), but the Messenger renamed him as

---
[1] Migration of the Prophet (s) and his companions from Mecca to Medina.
[2] The two shaykhs; i.e. Imam Bukhari & Imam Muslim.

Abdullah (Slave of Allah) after he embraced Islam – as recounted in *Siyar A'lam Al-Nubala'*[3] (Lives of the Noble Luminaries).

In actuality, he was nicknamed as *As-Siddeq* (the truthful one) since the Age of Ignorance (*Jahiliyya*), but the name cemented itself in Islam when the polytheists of Mecca notified him with the strange news that the Prophet ﷺ was claiming – the *Isra wa al-Mi'raj* – he's travelling to Masjid Al-Aqsa in Jerusalem and ascent to the Highest Heaven in a single night. To which Abu Bakr ؓ replied, 'If he has said that, then it is as he says.'

As for A'isha's mother, she is Umm Rumaan ؓ, known more famously by this nickname than her actual name, most likely Zaynab, but it has also be said it was Da'ad daughter of Amir. Her lineage goes back to Kinanah.

She was one of the earliest people to enter Islam. Sayidah A'isha ؓ says: 'I don't remember my parents except as Muslims.' Umm Rumaan ؓ lived until the caliphate of Uthman ؓ, not, as some have claimed, that she died in the 6th year hijri.[4]

Sayidah A'isha ؓ also had a brother from Umm Rumaan ؓ with the name Abdul Rahman. And she also had half-brothers and sisters from other mothers:

---

[3] Recounts the biographies of noble Muslims. Authored by Imam Al-Dhahabi (d. 749 hijri/1374 C.E)
[4] See Fath al-Bari, 7/337.

Abdullah, Asma', Muhammad and Umm Kulthum.

Sayidah A'isha ﷺ enjoyed a joyful childhood, as she narrated herself, playing and participating with her peers. And she continued doing so until she became a bride and the Prophet ﷺ married her. She says about herself, in what is narrated in the books of Bukhari and Muslim, "Umm Rumaan came to me while I was on a swing and with me were my friends. She shouted out to me and so I went up to her. And while I had no idea what she wanted, she grasped me by the hand until she stopped me at the door of the house. After I had caught my breath, she took me inside where I was surprised to see women from the Ansar. And they said "Best wishes and blessings, may you have your share of good…"

ENGAGEMENT AND MARRIAGE WITH THE MESSENGER

The first stage of the engagement of the Messenger to A'isha began with prophetic inspiration revealed to him. Both Bukhari and Muslim narrate in their authentic books that A'isha states:

'The Messenger of Allah said: I saw you in my dream three nights. An angel came to me with you wrapped in a piece of majestic, silken cloth and said, 'This is your wife'. I removed the piece of cloth from your face and there you were. I said to myself: If it is from Allah, then it will surely be.' It appears that this dream happened in the time of Khadijah .

Afterwards, Khawlah bint Hakeem , came to the Messenger after the passing of Khadijah and said to him, 'O Messenger of Allah, will you not marry?'

He replied, 'And to whom?'

She said, 'Do you want an unmarried woman or one that was married before?'

He replied, 'Who is the unmarried one and who is the one who was married before?'

She answered, 'As for the unmarried one, she is A'isha,

daughter of the most beloved of Allah's creation to you. As for the one that was married, it is Sawdah ibn Zama' – she has believed in you and follows you.'

He replied, 'Go to both and mention me to them.' (i.e., propose on my behalf).

So, she went to the house of Abu Bakr ﷺ, where she found Umm Rumaan ﷺ and said to her, 'What blessings and goodness have come down upon you!'

'How so?' Umm Rumaan ﷺ replied.

'The Messenger of Allah ﷺ has sent me on his behalf, to propose for A'isha.'

Umm Rumaan ﷺ said, "I would like you to wait for Abu Bakr to return."

Abu Bakr ﷺ came and she put the matter before him. But he said, 'Is it right when A'isha is the daughter of his brother?'

So Khawlah ﷺ returned and mentioned that to the Prophet ﷺ. To which he replied, 'Tell Abu Bakr: You are my brother in Islam (not by blood) and so marriage to your daughter is permissible for me.'

So, Abu Bakr ﷺ gave her in marriage to him ﷺ and she was six or seven years old.

However, the marriage remained as an engagement or contract only. The Prophet ﷺ did not marry her proper nor live with her until the second year after the hijra when she moved into the room he prepared for her.

As for Sawdah ؓ, the Prophet ﷺ married her in the tenth year after his receiving prophethood, that is, about three years before his marriage with A'isha ؓ.

When the Prophet ﷺ made hijra[5] with Abu Bakr ؓ, Sayidah Aisha ؓ remained back with those that also delayed their hijra from the families of the Prophet ﷺ and Abu Bakr ؓ. They were not able to catch up with the Prophet ﷺ until later. The family of Abu Bakr ؓ, and foremost among them A'isha ؓ, endured some difficulties and dangers in their journey towards Medina.

When they settled in the city of Medina, they were touched by its plague. The city at the time was named Yathrib (a name which carries a negative connotation in Arabic). It was known for its harsh climate and many of them fell sick. Amongst them was Abu Bakr ؓ, A'isha ؓ and others.

When the Prophet ﷺ saw their state, he called upon Allah ﷻ, saying, 'O Allah...make Medina beloved to us like you have made Mecca beloved to us...or yet make it more beloved and improve it for

---

[5] Migration from Mecca, after the persecution of Muslims there, to the city of Mecca. [Tr.]

us and bless it in its Saa' and Madd (its small and large, great and little) and remove its fever and move it away to *al-Juhfa* (a desolate location)'.

Allah ﷻ certainly did accept the prayer of His Messenger ﷺ and the climate of Medina became agreeable soon after, and even became the most delightful cities of Allah ﷻ and He purified it of its plague.

Sayidah A'isha ﷺ became healthy again after the passing of a month. She had lost weight and even her hair was falling off, but health and soundness returned to her soon after.

The Prophet ﷺ completed his marriage with her in the second year of the hijri calendar, after the Battle of Badr, in the month of Shawwal – according to the soundest hadith reporters. A'isha ﷺ would say, 'The Prophet performed the marriage contract with me in the month of Shawwal and began living with me in the month of Shawwal, then which of the wives of the Prophet was more favoured by him as me!?'[6]

Her dowry received from the Prophet ﷺ was five hundred dirhams as Imam Muslim ﷺ narrates in his authentic collection of hadith.

Sayidah A'isha ﷺ has described the bed in the room in which she moved into. She says, 'Indeed,

---

6 Sayidah A'isha was pointing to the importance of Shawwal with Muslims, since it contains the Eid festival after Ramadan.

the mattress of the Messenger on which he slept was tanned skin stuffed with palm fibres'. Imam Bayhaqi narrates that A'isha said, 'A women from the Ansar visited me and she saw the mattress of the Messenger as a folded sheet. So, she sent to me a mattress that was filled with cotton.

When the Prophet chanced upon it he said, 'What is this O A'isha?'

She replied, 'O Messenger of Allah, so and so from the Ansar came and saw your mattress so she went out and sent this one to me.'

The Prophet said, 'Send it back to her O A'isha. If I wanted from the riches of Allah, then with me would be mountains of gold and silver.'

A REBUTTAL TO THE FALSEHOOD SPREAD AGAINST THIS MARRIAGE.

Some people have spoken foolishly in our times, about the marriage of the Messenger of Allah ﷺ with A'isha ﷺ. They exaggerate the issue, saying that the Messenger of Allah ﷺ, being 53 years of age, married a small girl not older than 9. Perhaps some others may claim that this was an evil decision that came about from an oppressive personality.

But words such as this, don't arise except from someone with a sense of honour or concern for A'isha ﷺ, from someone who cares that she not be oppressed or suffer from such a marriage. Otherwise, there is no reason to raise condemnation or criticism about it.

Now is there any historian or translator, historically or in the modern era, who has uncovered a shred of evidence, or even a suspicion of evidence that A'isha ﷺ was made miserable by that marriage or that she was forced into accepting it? But rather, is there any historian or biographer that doesn't know that A'isha ﷺ was the happiest of all women in Madinah with her husband? Rather, her happiness and love for the Messenger of Allah ﷺ has become a parable and oft-quoted point. What then is the purpose of these critics to circulate with such emphasis their condemnation of this marriage?

Indeed, a man shoving his nose in what doesn't concern him and what he cannot understand comes in many, different forms. But you will not find it stirred up in a more despicable way or a more degrading and ugly manner than this form. What is the meaning of these people condemning a marriage, in which A'isha ﷺ, being its bride, was the happiest person with it!? What is the source of their exaggeration against a fortune, about which A'isha ﷺ continued to boast about until the end of her life?

Let us consider what the source of this criticism is. How can these commentators disapprove of a marriage while its bride was the happiest of people with it!?

The source of it is that these criticisers don't believe that Muhammad ﷺ has any merit or advantage over any other distinguished man from the Arabian Peninsula. That no Prophethood or Message or Divine Revelation came down amongst them. Just delusions that drove those that believed in him to believe in him. Or that it was all a fabrication that Muhammad ﷺ found good and well to take up as an occupation for himself, like some of them have claimed. However, it was A'isha's ﷺ certainty of knowledge, as well as her parent's, that Muhammad ﷺ, being the Messenger to all mankind from Allah ﷻ, was distinguished by Allah ﷻ with qualities, characteristics, and capabilities that honoured him above all mankind. This certainty, supported by clear evidence, is the secret to her happiness and that of her family's with this marriage.

What type of logic is this, that those criticisers believe, gives them the right to impose their conclusions upon everyone who disagrees with them in the matter of the Prophethood of Muhammad ﷺ? And what logic – if it can be called logic – agrees with these deniers to allow them to have such authority over others? Would those deniers accept that others be given the same standard of judgement over their own beliefs? Where is the freedom of speech that is supposed to protect thoughts, beliefs, and aspirations from holders of such narrow opinions and lovers of injustice?

They believe that since they have denied the prophethood of the Messenger of Allah ﷺ as well as the rare and great virtues that necessitate from it, and since they have denounced this marriage, all people, and at the forefront, A'isha ؓ and her family must also denounce this marriage just like they have! Also, she must then reject the happiness she felt in the house of Prophethood and deny it, out of respect to the criticism of this strange group and to be in unity with them!

We can take such worthless talk seriously when we hear that it is rational to give this group authority over the belief's of everyone else as well as snatching from others their right minds and God-given free thought.

Subsequently, I received a letter during the supervision of the publishing of this book, from a friend from the United States of America. It contained a discussion between him and someone who simply went by the name 'Mike' over the internet. In fact, I received it just as I was reviewing the passages on the marriage of the Messenger of Allah ﷺ with Sayidah A'isha ؓ and the falsehood spoken by deceivers concerning it. The letter is worthy of attention and arouses astonishment. As you will now see.

This 'Mike' focuses his discussion on what he calls: 'The condemnation of the marriage of the Messenger with a child nine years old based on sound human nature.'

The discussion concludes with Mike saying that the marriage of the Messenger of Allah ﷺ with a girl still playing with dolls, is not consistent with a sound human nature. Perhaps Mike has relied on fabricated reports that some perjurers have concocted against Islamic history and the life of the Prophet of Allah ﷺ. One of these fabrications is that Muhammad ﷺ began dreaming about his marriage with Sayidah A'isha ؓ since she was between four and five years old. And they try to paste this slander into Sahih Bukhari!

Mike says maybe what drove the Messenger of Allah ﷺ to marry A'isha at that age was signs of psychological disease. He questions my friend through the internet, 'Would you agree that a man, fifty years of age, sleeps with a girl aged nine? If you do not agree, then you are a hypocrite, because your religion allows this. However, if you do agree, then all I can say is that I know many people who would desire to seek you out and your religion, to marry your young girls that have not yet reached nine years of age.'

To you, dear reader, I share this rebuttal which I directed to this Mike, through my friend who showed me his words and objections.

Firstly. We do not find in Sahih Bukhari or other hadith books, that the Messenger of Allah ﷺ dreamt of the wedding with A'isha ؓ at the time her age was four or five, which was before the death of Khadija ؓ. No doubt, it is just the shameless fabrication of lies upon the book of Bukhari and an invented distortion against the station of the Messenger of Allah ﷺ and his elevated, personal character and status. If not that, then it is a rejected forgery and contradiction to what the two shaykhs – Bukhari and Muslim – have narrated in their authenticated hadith collections that A'isha ؓ reports that the Messenger of Allah ﷺ said to her, 'I dreamt about you three nights, an angel came to me with you wrapped in silk. He said this is your wife. I uncovered your face and behold it was you! I said to myself if this is from Allah, then He will make it come to pass.'

I do not rule out that this foolish slander,

which has no basis, is an incorrect translation relying on this hadith which one cannot understand except in the context of revelation and prophethood and when one knows that Muhammad ﷺ is the Messenger of Allah ﷻ to all humankind and that he is supported by revelation from Allah ﷻ.

Secondly. Muhammad ﷺ did not choose for himself, amongst other girls, this young one, Sayidah A'isha ﷺ. Nor did he before that, have any association with her. Further, he did not go personally to her parents to insist they marry her to him. No one has claimed as such from those dedicated to the history and the biography of the Prophet ﷺ.

Rather, what occurred was what is narrated in Bukhari and other books that Khawlah bint Hakeem ﷺ went to the Messenger of Allah ﷺ and said: O Messenger of Allah, will you not marry?

He said: To whom?

She replied: Do you want an unmarried one or one that was married before?

He asked: Who is the unmarried and who is the previously married?

She replied: As for the unmarried, then it is A'isha, daughter of the most beloved of Allah's creation to you. As for the previously married one, it is Sawdah bint Zama'h, she has believed in you and follows you.

30 - A REBUTTAL TO THE FALSEHOOD SPREAD AGAINST THIS MARRIAGE.

He said: Then go to them both and mention me to them... (until the end of the hadith).

So, the Messenger of Allah ﷺ had no intention of even seeking a young woman beforehand. The only thing that pointed A'isha ؓ out to him and suggested her to him, was the question of Khawlah ؓ. All the matter was, was that she introduced the idea to him and he tentatively agreed. Then from whence the perception that the Messenger of Allah ﷺ suffered from any mental sickness?

The approval of Khawlah ؓ that A'isha ؓ be the wife of the Messenger ﷺ and her proposing her to him, and in the agreement of her parents without hesitation[7], points to the fact that this idea did not induce any criticism from anyone in the Meccan population generally and neither in its Muslim community specifically.

And yet we know that if this proposal had any hint of breaching sound human nature – which Mr. Mike alleges – the shouts of its objectors would have been found aplenty. Particularly since, most of the people of Mecca at that time were the primary enemies

---

[7] The reply of Abu Bark (r) to Khawlah (r) when she came to propose for A'isha to the Messenger of Allah (s) of - 'Is it right for him when she is the daughter of his brother?' – was not a rejection of the proposal itself. Rather it was Abu Bakr's belief at the time that the brotherhood of faith that was fastened between himself and the Messenger (s), would make the Messenger (s) the uncle of A'isha and hence be a prohibited relationship. Hence, the Prophet (s) said to him, 'You are my brother in Islam' (i.e., not a blood-brother).

to Muhammad ﷺ, the protagonist of this proposal.

Thirdly. If Mike responds by saying that no weight should be given to the consent of the Meccan society for this type of marriage as a sound human nature does not approve a fifty-three-year-old marrying a nine-year-old girl, then the response which ought to not be absent from Mike's mind and neither from the mind of anyone who is blessed with nuanced knowledge and culture is: The age-range of physical maturity in young girls varies with differences in environment and climate. In hot countries like Arabia and many African countries, girls reach the age of puberty and physical maturity at an early age – it is commonplace in Egypt, for example, where girls are known to reach puberty at the age of ten. It can also be observed in places like Sudan and Nigeria. This contrasts with countries with colder climates, such as Central Asia and many European countries where girls may arrive at fourteen years of age, without reaching puberty.

This is the explanation of the reaction of the Meccan society to the proposal of the Messenger of Allah ﷺ to Sayidah A'isha ﷺ. They accepted it wholly and voluntarily. They would not approve of a practice unknown to them, but it was what was in natural harmony with the climate and environment.

However, it is likely Mike would respond by saying: Supposing the matter is so, is it not oppressive for a man, whose long years have withered the flower of his life and has absorbed or is about to absorb all its liveliness, to marry a young girl who has met life anew and still blossoming?

The answer, which too is not absent from any objective researcher, is that the distinction between what is oppressive and what is not, is not revealed by my sentiments or that of Mike's towards this matter, who are not involved with it in any way. Neither are we the ones to say that profit or loss came from it. This distinction can only be revealed by the sentiments and feelings of the bride and her family, who had a connection and direct involvement in the matter.

Indeed, it is love or hatred of the wife or husband that are the judges in such a matter, not the assumptions and imaginings of interfering meddlers. If the feelings of Sayidah A'isha towards her marriage with Prophet Muhammad were made to be known to Mike, he would be convinced that she was living the life of the happiest wife in the world. She, in fact, herself made this clear on multiple occasions. Then what is the value of the feelings of others when they have absolutely no idea of the sentiments of the actual wife of the marriage!?

Edward VIII abdicated from the throne of England, relinquishing all its benefits and inheritances, in the path of love for a woman who was – as they say – not the most beautiful woman and had been divorced twice before. Would this Mike, use the same argument, which he uses to deceive people, over the interests of Edward and his happiness and the love which had overpowered his heart? (That is to denounce such a marriage while ignoring the feelings of those involved – Tr.)

Edward VIII only loved a woman for her body and soul, but those who love Muhammad ﷺ do so because of their love for the Greatest and only Lord, Allah, Glorious and Magnanimous. How then, can any of us suppose that Mike possesses some imaginary concern for the interests of Sayidah A'isha ؓ and use it as an argument that overpowers the argument of her longing heart filled with love for the Messenger of Allah ﷺ, who was sent as a mercy to all the worlds?!

Fourthly. Mike's comparison of the people he knows with the Messenger of Allah ﷺ, that they should be allowed to marry young Muslim girls from our Islamic society, is an analogy with a tremendous dissimilarity.

In other words, the marriage proposal of a person in the position of Muhammad ﷺ, the Messenger of Allah ﷺ to the entire world, to a Muslim girl of the age of A'isha ؓ, would be a cause of honour and happiness for her and her family, without doubt. This would only need one condition – the certainty of this family that this suitor, was truly blessed with that lofty station.

And given that there is not in the world any man who can ascend to the status which Muhammad was blessed with; the Seal of the Messengers and Prophets to mankind, then this condition is not applied to anyone except him alone till the establishment of the last hour.

I know that Mr. Mike does not concede any importance to this condition. For the Muhammad ﷺ, we know, is certainly the Messenger of God. But to him is naught but an ordinary man like those around him. He believes that those whom he tempts to marry young Muslim girls are like Muhammad ﷺ! However, I, like any Muslim, am certain with the prophethood of Muhammad ﷺ and his lofty rank with Allah ﷻ. On my part, I do not give any regard to the ignorance of this condition.

Therefore, the difference between us, which prevents us agreeing on one conclusion, is that Mike doesn't see in the person of Muhammad ﷺ more than an Arab man who had invented the claim of prophethood amongst his people. Rather, perhaps Mike's heart is not yet free, like many of his contemporaries, of hatred or jealousy against Muhammad ﷺ. However, we Muslims have firm conviction that he is the Master of the Prophets and Messengers and the last of them sent to the entire world and that many previous Prophets had informed their people of his coming and of his great station.

It is obvious that each position has its own rationalising and pre-conceived notions in understanding and evaluating this matter. The most obvious sign of this is that if a day comes in which Mike believes that Muhammad ﷺ was indeed the Messenger of Allah ﷻ to all humanity about whom, Moses ؑ and Jesus ؑ gave good tidings of his coming, and that he was supported by revelation from Allah ﷻ, then this confusion would be absent from his mind and this argument which he argues with would disappear. Then, the outlook which I have just expressed would take its place completely. Just like many others, who embraced Islam, farewelled their previous imaginings and prejudiced convictions without returning to them.

I say lastly to Mike:
The day you think objectively…and are sure that Muhammad ﷺ was not a pretender amongst men and neither did he deceive them when he presented himself as a Prophet sent to all mankind from the Nurturing Lord of the Worlds, and the day you look at him, rather to his biography, with the eye of his companions that were around him, then you will know that it was Allah ﷻ who chose for his Messenger this young girl. Just as the Messenger ﷺ related to A'isha ؓ in the hadith earlier mentioned (when he saw her in a regal cloth presented to him by an angel – Tr.). You would be certain that in this Divine choice there are wisdoms. And you would congratulate A'isha ؓ with all your heart with this distinguishing goodness and happiness that descended upon her.

IN THE HOUSE OF PROPHETHOOD

Sayidah A'isha ﷺ entered the house of Prophethood as a wife to our master Muhammad ﷺ still with her youthfulness. The Prophet ﷺ attended to her like only the best husband would, all the while keeping in mind her young age and needs and ensured that her setting was agreeable to her.

It appears in the authentic hadith collections, that the Prophet ﷺ would send her friends to her to keep her company. He would let her place her head on his shoulder while being hidden behind him to watch the Abyssinians put on a show with their spears in the masjid. Sayidah A'isha ﷺ mentions:
'It was the day of Eid and Africans were show-fighting with their shields and spears. Either I asked the Prophet ﷺ or he asked me whether I would like to see. I said yes. So, he raised me up behind him, my cheek by his cheek saying, 'Carry On! O tribe of Irfida!' (We remained like that) until I got bored and he said, 'You've had enough'[8].

Sayidah A'isha ﷺ occupied a deep place of love in the heart of the Messenger ﷺ, which the other Mothers of the Believers[9] did not reach. Perhaps this at times stirred jealously with the other Mothers of the Believers.

---

8 Agreed upon hadith. Wording of Imam Bukhari.
9 The title and station given to the wives of the Prophet ﷺ.

The people used to send presents to the Prophet ﷺ on the day of A'isha's turn. A'isha ؓ relates, "My companions (i.e., the other wives of the Prophet) gathered in the house of Um Salama ؓ (the wife of the Prophet) and said, "O Um Salama! By Allah, the people choose to send presents on the day of A'isha's turn and we too, love the good (i.e., gifts etc.) as A'isha does. You should tell Allah's Messenger (s) to tell the people to send their presents to him wherever he may be, or wherever his turn may be." Um Salama ؓ mentioned that to the Prophet ﷺ and he turned away from her. She repeated it again and the Prophet ﷺ again turned away and when she told him for the third time, the Prophet ﷺ said, "O Um Salama! Don't trouble me regarding A'isha, for by Allah, Divine Revelation never came to me while I was with any woman amongst you except her."[10]

And Sayidah A'isha ؓ would ask the Messenger ﷺ, "How is your love for me?"

He would reply, 'Like a knot in a rope.'

She said, from then on, I would ask him, 'How is the knot, O Messenger of Allah?'

To which he would reply, 'It is as it was.'

Also from the authentic traditions, the Messenger ﷺ said to Sayidah Fatima, may the Good-Pleasure of Allah be upon her, 'O my daughter. Do

---
10 Bukhari.

you not love whom I love?

She replied, 'Of course.'

He said, 'I love this one' – and pointed towards Sayidah A'isha ﷺ.

Amr ibn al-As ﷺ at one point questioned the Messenger ﷺ, 'Who is the most beloved of people to you?'

He replied, 'A'isha.'

He said, 'And from the men?'

He replied, 'Her father.'

It was known amongst the Companions ﷺ, how strong the love of the Messenger ﷺ for A'isha ﷺ was. Some referred to her as the beloved of the Messenger of Allah ﷺ. It is reported by Tirmidhi, that a man spoke negatively of A'isha ﷺ in front of Ammar ibn Yasir ﷺ. Ammar replied to him, 'Be silent, despised and rejected! Do you insult the beloved of the Messenger of Allah ﷺ?'

At the forefront of those who recognised and appreciated this distinguishing quality, this special place that Sayidah A'isha ﷺ held in the heart of the Messenger of Allah ﷺ, was Sayidah Fatimah ﷺ – the daughter of the Prophet ﷺ. She would favour A'isha ﷺ due to this and due to this rank, which the other wives of the Prophet ﷺ perhaps had not reached. It was to A'isha ؓ that Fatima ؓ revealed the secret that the Messenger ﷺ parted to her shortly before his passing. She did not reveal it to anyone except A'isha ؓ.

Both Bukhari and Muslim narrate the hadith, in which A'isha ؓ states: The Prophet ﷺ whispered something to Fatima ؓ which made her cry intensely. When he saw her sadness, he whispered something to her a second time, which made her laugh.' When the Prophet ﷺ got up and left I asked her, 'What was it that the Messenger of Allah ﷺ said to you?' She replied, 'I will not reveal the secret of the Messenger of Allah ﷺ.'

After the Prophet ﷺ passed away, I again asked her, 'I beg you by what right I have over you to tell me what the Messenger of Allah said to you! – Upon him and his family be peace.'

Sayidah Fatima ؓ replied, 'Now, I will. As for the first time he whispered, he informed me that the angel Jibril ؑ would revise the Qur'an with him every year once or twice. He had revised it now twice (already). He said, "Truly, I don't see any reason for this hastening (in revising the Qur'an) except that my death has drawn near. So, keep Allah in mind and show patience, for it will be best for you that I precede you in this matter." And so, I cried how you saw me cry. When he ﷺ saw my grief, he whispered the second time saying, "O Fatimah, would you not be gladdened that you are the leader of believing women or the leader of women from this ummah (nation)?" So, I laughed how you saw me laugh.'[11]

It is enough to realise this cordiality between A'isha and Fatimah, if you ponder over the words of the former to the latter namely, 'I beg you by what right I have over you to tell me what the Messenger of Allah said to you!'

This privilege which A'isha enjoyed and was distinguished by did not prevent the Prophet from being just and fair with his interactions with his other wives. It has been established that he would treat them all equally in his interactions, to the extent that he would cast lots between them when he would travel. The wife winning the luck of the draw would be the one who would accompany him on that particular journey. After he would treat them justly, he would say, 'O Allah, this is (how I judge) to deal out with what I possess, blame me not for what You possess and not I'[12] (i.e., perfect justice).

***

Perhaps from the most significant reasons of this love, with which Sayidah A'isha distinguished herself above her co-wives, was what Allah favoured her with of merits and virtues, not gathered in anyone beside her.

---
11 Agreed upon. Shortened wording of Muslim.
12 Tirmidhi, Kitab ul-Nikah

The most prominent of which, was her being blessed with the art of eloquence, possessing superb literature and brilliance of expression.

Look to her words to the Messenger ﷺ, when he asked her permission, one night, if he could leave her bed to stand and pray to his Lord. She replied, 'Indeed I love being close to you, but I prefer your wishes over mine.'

And look to the artistry of her exposition on the day when the Messenger ﷺ said to her, 'I can tell when you are happy with me and when you are angry with me.'

'And how have you come to know that?' She replied.

The Messenger ﷺ answered, 'When you are happy with me, then (when you vow) you say – By the Lord of Muhammad! And when you are angry you say – By the Lord of Abraham!'
A'isha ؓ replied, 'Truly, O Messenger of Allah, the most I can leave from you is your name…'[13]

Further, she took interest in knowledge of the laws of Islam as well as memorisation and narration of the hadith of the Messenger of Allah ﷺ – showing excellence in both understanding and narrating. I hope to mention, if Allah grants success, some examples of her correcting the Companions ؓ in

---

13 Bukhari, Kitab al-Nikah, Bab Gheerat ul-Nisa'.

their understandings of some point of Islamic law or in the narration of a particular hadith.

And then there was her abundance of worship and devotion. It is evident she profited much from the example of the Messenger ﷺ, who would perform a large portion of his prayers in her room. She was blessed with continual performance of the late-night prayer (*qiyaam*), would fast regularly, and showed indifference to the material things of this world, applying what the Messenger ﷺ advised her. He once said to her, 'If you desire closeness with me, then it would suffice you to have from this world, the rations of a rider. Beware of sitting with the rich and do not consider a garment worn out till you have patched it.'[14]

Yet her observance of the Prophet's ﷺ advice did not prevent her from continuously adorning herself for the Messenger ﷺ and taking care of her appearance for him so that he would not see from her except what was pleasing.

It has been narrated by Abu Dawud from Sayidah A'isha ؓ : The Messenger ﷺ entered my room and saw two silver rings in my hand. He asked, 'What is this, A'isha?'
I replied, 'I have made them as ornaments to wear for you, O Messenger of Allah.'
'Have you paid zakat (charity) on them?'
I replied, 'No or whatever Allah has willed.'

---

14 At-Tirmidhi, Kitab al-Libas.

He replied, 'It is sufficient to take you to the Fire.'[15]

She would advise women to adorn themselves for their husbands. She mentioned to one of them, 'If you have a husband and you could remove your eyes and set them back better than before, then do so!'[16]

The Messenger's love for Sayidah A'isha continued and increased until his passing. In fact, this love perhaps manifested itself shortly before his death, like never before.

When the Messenger was suffering from the sickness which led to his passing, he would ask as he would go from one wife's home to another's, 'Where will I be tomorrow? Where will I be after tomorrow?' He would ask this yearning to return to Sayidah A'isha. The Mothers of the Believers agreed that the Messenger ought to be nursed where he prefers and gave him permission to stay in A'isha's house.[17]

And so, the Prophet's wish was fulfilled and he was moved to the house of Sayidah A'isha, who watched over him and nursed him until he moved on to the final abode.

Sayidah A'isha describes these final moments of their time together:

---

15 Abu Dawud, Kitab al-Zakat.
16 Al-Sayidah A'isha, Abdul Hameed Tahmaaz quoting Siyar A'lam Al-Nubala'.
17 Saheeh Muslim, Kitab Fadl A'isha.

'Truly did Allah unite between my spittle and the spittle of the Messenger at the time of his death. Abdul Rahman (her brother) came into the room and in his hand was a miswak. I was acting as a pillow for the Messenger and I saw him look towards it and I knew how much he loved the miswak. So, I asked him, "Shall I take it for you?" He gestured yes with his head. I handed it over to him but he found it rough. "Shall I soften it for you?" I asked him. He again gestured yes. I took it, chewed it and cleaned it making it suitable for him. I passed it over to him again and he brushed his teeth with it – the best I ever saw him brush his teeth. Then he was about to pass it back to me but his hand fell and I began to pray for him with the prayer that the Angel Gabriel ﷺ would pray for him. The Messenger ﷺ would also pray for himself with it when he became sick. Suddenly, he raised his sight to the heavens and said – *Al-Rafeeq Al-A'la!* (i.e., I choose to be with The Highest Friend) – then his soul issued forth.'

Sayidah A'isha ﷺ would say, 'All praise belongs to Allah, who united between my spittle and the Prophet's ﷺ spittle on his last day in this world.'[18]

***

Yet what was the level of her living standards with the Messenger ﷺ under the shade of this love?

One may think she enjoyed a life of ease

---
18 Musnad Imam Ahmed, 6/48

and affluence. That the Messenger ﷺ would spend abundantly on her in accordance with his love, with all manner of pleasures and luxuries.

It was however, on the contrary. She once mentioned to her nephew, Urwa ؓ, the circumstances of her day to day living, 'O my nephew. We would look to the new moon, then another, then yet another. Three moons would pass (i.e., three months) and no fire was kindled in the house of the Messenger of Allah (for cooking).
He asked, 'Then what would sustain you?'
She answered, 'The two black things. Dates and water.'[19]

On describing the conditions in the house of the Messenger ﷺ on the day of his passing, she mentions, 'The Messenger of Allah passed away and there was nothing edible in my house to eat other than some barley on my shelf. And I ended up eating from it for many days after.'

The Mothers of the Believers, Sayidah A'isha included, at one point complained about such harshness of livelihood involved with living with the Prophet ﷺ. They asked the Messenger ﷺ that their expenditures be increased to at least the level of the poorest wives of the Companions ؓ. This upset the Prophet ﷺ and he separated himself from their

---

[19] Al-Bukhari, Kitab Al-Riqaaq. (Water in a vessel in poorly lit home would undoubtedly appear black. That might be the reason Sayidah A'isha referred to it as black).

company for some time. It was then that Allah ﷻ revealed the verses upon His Messenger:

'O (Esteemed) Prophet! Say to your wives: 'If you long for this world and its glitter, then come! I shall make a provision for you and set you free in a handsome manner. But if you long for Allah and His Messenger and the abode of the Hereafter, then surely Allah has prepared for the pious amongst you a tremendous reward.'[20]

The Prophet ﷺ called his wives and recited upon them these two options stipulated by Allah ﷻ – either accepting their request of betterment in their living standards but separating from the Prophet ﷺ or patiently persevering with the Prophet's ﷺ abstinence, frugality and coarseness of living – thereby earning abundant reward and unimaginable compensation in the Hereafter.

The Prophet ﷺ began with our mother, A'isha ﷺ. He presented her the choice, 'I will mention a matter to you in which you must not hurry to decide, until you consult your parents.' When had presented the Decree of Allah ﷻ, she replied, 'Am I to consult my parents about you!? No, rather I choose Allah and His Messenger and the home of the Hereafter.'[21] The rest of his wives also made the same decision.

---

20 Quran; Surah Ahzab [33:28-29]
21 Bukhari. Also Muslim with similar wording.

A SIDENOTE: THE SACRED MEANING OF THE PROPHET'S LOVE FOR WOMEN.

Among people today are those who are content with holding a depraved understanding of love. It is not far-fetched that if they listen to our words, they can only imagine the love of the Messenger ﷺ for Sayidah A'isha ﷺ and the rest of his wives, in accordance with the pre-conceived ideas and notions lodged in their minds.

Then, on the other hand, there are those who are superficially learned in Islam, who would turn a blind eye to much of what we have mentioned, even disregard it, so they don't render themselves embarrassed in front of others. From the narrowness of their perception, there seems to be no explanation for such controversial issues. Perhaps they would disregard, because of their resignation, a famous and authentic hadith like the saying of the Messenger of Allah ﷺ, 'Two things have been made dear to me from your world – perfume and women. But in the midst of prayer has been placed the apple of my eye.' The consequence of disregarding this hadith is even worse than what they imagine of shame in front of their contemporaries.

The reality, however, is not hidden from any thinker who ponders upon the biography of the

Messenger ﷺ as a whole, from beginning to end. This trait, which we know of in the Messenger ﷺ, that is, his affection for women, makes clear in front of all eyes, a virtue from amongst his most honourable qualities. It allows us to marvel at his unprecedented and elevated humanity and purity of nature. It unveils an important aspect of the messenger-ship of the Prophet ﷺ as an educator and teacher.

Now, we know that Muhammad ﷺ was only sent to complete perfect character as he mentioned about himself. And if we look at any action in one's life, it can be directed towards one of two possible directions. A direction that is evil and corrupt or one that is good and reforming. Certainly, the mission which Muhammad, the Chosen One ﷺ was sent with, was to tarry with people in the best, possible way – the way of goodness and reform in every relationship and in every aspect of his conduct. Whether from his verbal, advising speech to his elucidating behaviour and action.

When we consider the Arabs at the time of the Prophet ﷺ, we see they would go well and beyond acts of chivalry, generosity, and passion. However, they would do these in a manner that was corrupt and evil, not good and reforming. Likewise, they would greatly regard nobleness, but would abide by it, most of the time, again through its face of corruption. Yes, they were abound with feelings of love and passion for women, transcribing much of their emotions in fine poems of infatuation, reciting them during their physical relationships. But again, the problem was, that they would express this love through its evil face – that of selfishness, exploitation and despicableness.

That was so because the word 'love' for the average, pre-Islamic era Arabian, was used to just denote the fulfillment of his instinctual, sexual desires. To the extent that, once he had satisfied himself, he would treat a woman as an object thrown in the corner of his house, owned and not possessing, ordered about without her opinion being considered, busying herself with his needs while he would disregard hers. But then, when his instinctual desires were once again roused, he would return to the passionate chanting of rhymes, claiming his undying love, being led by his selfish desires, beneath the mask of yearning and romantic language. Until, having achieved his desire, would fling, what was now an object again, back to its storage spot to be treated the same as before. Women had become, like it was said about them – 'You are a game in the corner of the house, for the one who must fulfill his need to play with.'

And so, the Messenger of Allah ﷺ was dispatched to rectify what had been corrupted. To straighten such despicable attitudes and clarify the correct, humane conduct as opposed to inverted and corrupt notions and relationships. And perhaps, the proper relationship between husband and wife with the underlying love between them, is from the most important of notions to be rectified, in greatest need to be cared for and fostered.

50 - A SIDENOTE: THE SACRED MEANING OF THE PROPHET'S LOVE FOR WOMEN.

The mission of the Prophet ﷺ in correcting these notions and showing correct, humane, and social conduct, was not only through words and theoretical knowledge. Rather, it was also – more importantly – by way of example and being a role-model. This is the wisdom behind Allah ﷻ shaping the Prophet ﷺ in the best mould. Showing the method of perfect morals and character, sound social relationships and the control of natural, human desires within their proper and lawful limits.

Therefore, it was necessary – for it to be feasible for the Messenger ﷺ to correct the understanding of this love and show its humane and correct definition – that the Arabs, and mankind in general, witness from the Messenger ﷺ, clarification by way of example and proper conduct. Just like we learn from his general, moral character and relationships with others. In fact, we witness from him, the best path social life should follow in every age.

Hence, through the expression of his life, the perfect example of humane relationships between men and women in society becomes clear to us. As well as the relationship between a man and his wife. Just like the manner of all other social relationships and personal conduct was made evident through his example.

Indeed, our gazes are turned towards his example regarding his love for Sayidah A'isha ﷺ and the exclusivity of the relationship with her just as they are turned to his honouring of women generally when he said, 'Two things have been made beloved to me from your world – perfume and women. Yet the apple of my eye is found in prayer.' And when we follow our gazes, we find that he ﷺ puts us, via this love, in front of the most elevated and humane example for the relationship between men and women. We see that his love for Sayidah A'isha ؓ particularly, and for women generally, arose from his honouring them, elevating their status and sanctifying the peace and comfort which the hand of Divine Wisdom has weaved between them and their husbands.

Likewise, we observe and find the Prophet ﷺ translating this honour into the elevated social position he appointed women under the shade of Islam; they were consulted like men and followed in every sound opinion.

The Messenger ﷺ was first to consult them and they would give him their advice. They would engage in their own contracts with men and bring litigation against them on equal terms. They would inherit and bequeath and would earn a wage at the same rate as their male counterparts.

And we listen to him ﷺ as he voices and clarifies his honour and love for them when he says, 'Women are but the sisters of men. None honours them except the honourable and none disgraces them except the despicable.'²²

And he ﷺ says, 'The best of you are those best to their families and I am the best of you to my family.'²³

And he ﷺ said, 'Treat woman kindly...'²⁴

So, the Prophet's ﷺ love for women in general and particularly for Sayidah A'isha ؓ was clearly a practical means to clarify this proper regard men should have for women, directing man's nature and human instincts appropriately. The example, which Allah ﷻ made out of him ﷺ, as a source and leader of this proper relationship, is not realised by mere advice and hollow words, but only when its meanings are moulded into conduct and actions.

Now ponder over this practical approach and how it is an explanation for the Prophet's love for women and for Sayidah A'isha ؓ. Do you see in this love anything that blemishes or diminishes his moral conduct in any manner or contravenes any human right or noble virtues or any principles of Islam?

If this love grew out of personal desires and if he was one to satisfy worldly pleasures, then it would have been evident in the Prophet's ﷺ lifestyle and home. Then why do we observe the life of Sayidah

---

22 Musnad Imam Ahmed
23 Mustadarak Hakim.
24 Agreed upon in its authenticity.

A'isha ﷺ with him built upon the coarsest of living and great abstinence? And why did he give her and his other wives the choice between divorcing him and freeing themselves from such difficult living or remaining with him with patience? Truly, if we were to think the Messenger of Allah ﷺ was attached to this world, then he would have been foremost to please his wives with all the material pleasures of this world at his disposal, its goodly things, and in appeasing to their wishes.

If Islam could speak amongst men to introduce itself and disclose its most prominent feature, it would say that it is composed out of love…and if this love then spoke about its true nature, it would say its greatest manifestation was the love of the Messenger of Allah ﷺ.

THE SLANDER

In the city of Medina, there was a group of hypocrites who appeared to profess Islam but in actuality disbelieved. They thereby sought the benefits of Islam and its community and avoided the consequences of outward hostilities to it.

The head of this movement of hypocrisy was Abdullah ibn Ubay ibn Sulool, who had an alliance and amity with the Jewish tribes of Bani Nadheer and Bani Qaynuqa'.

When Bani Nadheer and Bani Qaynuqa' were expelled from Medina for their treacheries, it placed ibn Ubay in quite a bitter mood, as he was forced into alienation he didn't expect. He had pinned high hopes on these two tribes remaining in Medina.

He found no outlet for his gloom and grief except by trying whatever he could to harm the Messenger of Allah ﷺ, the Companions ﵏, the Ansar and Muhajireen. He was tireless in his efforts to stir up problems and harm whenever he saw an opportunity.

In the military skirmish of Bani Mustalaq in the month of Shabaan, 5th year after Hijra, a young servant of Umar ibn al-Khattab ﵁ quarrelled with an Ansari servant by a watering spot known as the Water of

Marisee, by the camp of the Muslims. Ibn Ubay (a native of Madinah) happened to hear their disagreement and shouted out (to the Meccan emigrant), 'You defy us in our own land!? By Allah, we don't see the leaders of Quraysh except as described by (the parable) – If you fatten your dog it will bite you! By Allah if we return to Medina, the honourable of us will expel the contemptible!'[25]

When these words reached the ears of the Messenger ﷺ, he overlooked them and pacified the uproar from amongst the Companions ؓ that called for his death. And so, Ibn Ubay's intrigues were put to rest for a while but that only increased him in spite and anguish. To make it worse, some of his allies disbanded from him on witnessing the clemency of the Messenger ﷺ, which outshone all expectations and conceptions of the time.

He went on looking for any way to harm the Messenger ﷺ, his grudge inflamed by his swift failures.

It wasn't long till he saw his opportunity. He seized on the news of what befell Sayidah A'isha ؓ during the return of the army of the

---

25 Tabaqaat ibn Sad. Tr. – Ibn Ubay was originally destined to be the leader of Medina before the arrival of the Prophet (s). These words seem to be an attack on the Messenger and Umar ibn al-Khattab as them being from the leading tribes of Quraish in Mecca, who had emigrated to Medina and destroyed Ibn Ubay's political aspirations in the process.

Messenger ﷺ from the skirmish of *Bani Mustalak*. Ibn Ubay took it upon himself to distort what he heard to defame Sayidah A'isha ؓ and accuse her of immorality. He hoped such a charge would permanently harm the Messenger ﷺ, quenching his thirst for revenge and compensate for his own humiliation and insult.

What was this piece of information? And how did Ibn Ubay take advantage of it for his own nefarious purposes?

Sayidah A'isha ؓ narrates, 'When the Prophet ﷺ was done with the skirmish, he announced the return (to Medina) and I went off to answer the call of nature. When I returned to the caravan, my hand fell to my chest and (I realised) my necklace had broken and fallen off. I returned to search for it and was kept busy in doing so. In the meantime, the party that was responsible for carrying my howdah[26] - and this was after the verses of hijab – picked it up, placed it on my camel, thinking I was inside. They urged the camel up and set off home. When I finally found my necklace and returned to camp, it was deserted, not a caller nor one to reply in sight. I headed for my original location, thinking they would find me missing and seek me there. Safwan ibn Muattal ؓ was following the army and passed by my spot seeing a black shape. He recognised me when he saw me, as he had seen me before hijab, and I covered my face with my clothes. By Allah, we spoke not a word to one another, nor

---

[26] A closed box carried on top of a camel to carry noble women – like our mother A'isha (r) – Tr.

did I hear him say anything other than his *istirjaa'* (exclaiming in astonishment – Truly to Allah we belong and to Him do we return!). He descended from his camel, made it kneel and I travelled on it as he led the camel by foot, until we reached the army that was sweltering in the heat of noon and chosen to camp. Then perished whoever perished (by making insinuations against me). And the one who assumed the greatest role in that slander was Abdullah ibn Ubay ibn Sulool.'

Sayidah A'isha also narrates, 'I became sick after reaching Medina for a whole month. All the while people where spreading the slander and I knew nothing of it. All that I noticed was that I wasn't receiving the same level of affection from the Messenger when I would usually get sick. He would just come and greet me and ask, "How are you?" When I had regained some health, I went out one night with Umm (mother of) Mistah to answer the call of nature as we didn't have a latrine. On the way back, Umm Mistah stumbled over her veil and swore, "May Mistah be ruined!"

I replied to her, "How terrible a thing you have said! Would you curse a man who witnessed the Battle of Badr!?"

She replied, "Have you not heard what he has said?"

And she informed me about the slander. And a sickness overpowered me on top of my sickness. And

I cried that night until it became day, my eyes could not melt any more tears nor be caressed by sleep."

The Messenger of Allah ﷺ began to consult some of his Companions on whether he should part from his family (i.e., from A'isha). Amongst them some said, "Hold firm to your family, we know only good from her". Others said, "Allah has not made things difficult upon you and women are aplenty. And question the servant girl – that is Barira ﷺ – she will tell you the truth." So, the Messenger ﷺ called for Barira ﷺ and asked her, "Have you seen anything that gives you reason to doubt A'isha?" She replied she knew nothing of A'isha except goodness.

The Messenger ﷺ then took to the minbar and said, "O community of believers! Who will relieve me from a man whose harm has the reached the people of my house (*ahl ul-Bayt*)? By Allah, I know nothing of my family except goodness. And they mention a man, who I also know to be nothing but righteous.'

Sa'ad ibn Muad ﷺ stood up and said, 'I will relieve him from you O Messenger of Allah. If he is from (the tribe of) 'Aws we will strike his neck. And if he be from (the tribe of) of Khazraj – then you have ordered us and we will fulfill your command.'

This caused a clamour of disagreement to be raised in the Masjid until they were silenced by the Messenger ﷺ.

Sayidah A'isha ؓ continues, 'Afterwards, the Prophet ﷺ came to visit me while my parents were with me. They were thinking my insides would burst from crying. The Prophet ﷺ had not sat with me since the slander had spread. Further, a month had passed by without him receiving any revelation clarifying the matter. He recited the declaration of faith as he sat down and said, "O A'isha. Such and such news has reached me about you. If you are innocent, then indeed Allah ﷻ will vindicate you. If you have committed a sin, then ask for Allah's Forgiveness and turn to Him in penitence."

When the Prophet ﷺ finished speaking, my tears dried up till I didn't sense a single teardrop remained and I said to my father, "Reply on my behalf to the Messenger of Allah ﷺ."

He replied, "By Allah, I don't know what to reply to him."

Then, I said to my mother, "Reply on my behalf."

She also said, "By Allah, I don't know what I should say."

So, I said, "By Allah, I know that you all heard such and such about me, until it became settled in your minds and you have now believed it. If I say to you that I am innocent – and Allah knows me as innocent – you would not believe me. But if I was to confess – then by Allah, who knows me as innocent, you would believe it. I do not find any advice for myself or for you except what the father of Prophet Yusuf ﷺ said: "**So better it is, to be steadfast (over this tragedy), and I seek only Allah's help against whatever you are narrating.**"²⁷

Then I turned away, laying down on my bed. By Allah, the Prophet ﷺ had not yet risen from his place, nor anyone else from the family had left, when Allah ﷻ send down revelation upon His Messenger ﷺ. He was overtaken by the usual agony and distress that accompanied revelation. Drops of perspiration would flow from him on a chilly winter's day from the weight of the Divine Words descending upon him. When this state passed him, he smiled and the first words he said were, "Glad tidings A'isha! As for Allah, he has declared your innocence."

My mother said to me, "Stand up for the Messenger (that is to thank him)."

I replied, "No, by Allah, I will not stand or thank anyone but Allah, for He is the One who vindicated me."'

The verses Allah (swt) revealed were: "**Truly those who brought forth the lie were a group among you. Do not suppose it to be an evil for you. Rather, it is a good for you. Unto each among them is the sin they committed. And he among them who undertook the greater part of it, his shall be a terrible torment.**

---

27 Quran; Surah Yousef (12:18)

Why, when you heard it, did not the believers, both men and women, think good of their own people and say: 'This is obviously a fabricated accusation'?

Why did these (*slanderers*) not produce four witnesses? For when they brought not the witnesses, it is they who were then liars in the sight of Allah.

And had there not been Allah's grace upon you and His mercy in this world and in the Hereafter, severe torment would have afflicted you for promoting that into which you rushed headlong.

When (*hearing this matter from one another*) you brought it on your tongues, and uttered with your mouths something about which you had no knowledge, and you took this matter as inconsiderable, whereas in the presence of Allah it was a grave (*offence underway*).

And when you heard this, why did you not declare (*at the same moment*): 'It is not for us to talk about it'? (*Rather you should have said: 'O Allah,*) Holy are You. This is a grave charge.'

Allah admonishes you to never repeat such a thing if you are believers.[28]

And Allah explains to you the Revelations with utmost clarity. And Allah is All-Knowing, All-Wise.

---

28 Quran, Surah Nur (24:11-21)

Indeed, those who like that lewdness should spread amongst the Muslims, for them is an agonising punishment in this world and in the Hereafter. And Allah knows (*the intentions of such people*)**, and you do not know.**

And had there not been Allah's grace and His mercy upon you (*you too would have been destroyed like the former communities*)**. But Allah is Most Clement, Ever Merciful.**

O believers! Do not follow the footsteps of Satan, and whoever follows the footsteps of Satan, then he (*Satan*) **certainly commands to practise** (*and promotes*) **immorality and sinful deeds. And if there had not been Allah's Grace and His Mercy upon you, then none of you would ever have been pure. But Allah purifies whom He wills, and Allah is All-Hearing, All-Knowing.**

Sayidah A'isha ﷺ continues, 'My father used to spend charity on Mistah (one of the propagators of the slander), because of their closeness of relation and of Mistah's poverty. So Abu Bakr ﷺ said, "By Allah, I will never spend anything on him again after what he said about A'isha. It was then that Allah ﷻ revealed the next verse:' **And** (*now*) **those of you who are exalted** (*by way of Religion*) **and are affluent** (*world wise*) **must not swear that they will not provide** (*financial help*) **to relatives, the needy and the Emigrants** (*who were involved in this offence*)**. They should forgive and**

overlook. Do you not like that Allah should forgive you? And Allah is Most Forgiving, Ever Merciful.²⁹

Upon hearing this, Abu Bakr ﷺ said, 'Rather I truly love that Allah would forgive me.' And he returned to donating to Mistah what he was accustomed to.

Then the Messenger ﷺ went out to the people and addressed them, reciting what Allah ﷻ had revealed from the Qur'an. The he ordered that Mistah ibn Uthatha, Hassan ibn Thabit and Hamnah ibna Jahsh be brought forward and whipped. They being the ones most vocal in spreading the slander.³⁰

***

After listening to the words of Sayidah A'isha ﷺ narrating her ordeal with this slander, it behoves us to analyse a few important points.

Firstly, it appears that this slander was a unique episode in the different designs used to cause harm to the Messenger ﷺ from his enemies. This affliction was most difficult on him as compared to all, previous afflictions. Thus was the nature of evil proceeding from the hypocrites. For they were always more far-reaching and effective in their plots and treacheries. Since they were facilitated by opportunities and

---

29 Quran, Surah Nur (24:22)
30 Narrated by Bukhari, Muslim, Ahmed, Ibn Majah, Abu Dawud and Ibn Ishaaq. With slight differences.

means not available to others.

All other misfortunes he ﷺ faced were expected, rather he was certain of them. He was predisposed to bear those burdens as advised by the Book of Allah ﷻ.

As for this slander, it was unanticipated. It confronted him ﷺ as a severe trial different from preceding ones. It was a rumour – something which could be true or false. If true, then it would be a painful stab in the most precious thing a man finds honour in. Yet how could his heart be at ease, how could he verify that it was false? From this perspective, the harm from it was more devastating in its effects. It would have put his inner, human feelings in uneasiness.

More crucially, if revelation had hastened down to reveal the reality of the matter and expose the hypocrites, he would have found refuge from this agitation and troubling doubt. Yet revelation, for whatever wisdom, went over a month without commenting anything on this rumour – yet another cause for concern.

Secondly, it is apparent that this trial, concealed great Divine Wisdom. It revealed a radiant proof of prophethood in the person of Muhammad ﷺ and how his conveyance of his message was free from anything that may taint it.

People of doubt and suspicion may have

continued to view the nature of prophethood as something coming mixed with the ideas of the Prophet ﷺ himself. The event of this slander, which separated one aspect of him, as being a man from amongst men, from the other aspect – of pure and true prophethood within him, manifested revelation perfectly in front of eyes and minds, so there remained no place for ambiguity between it and any possible personal addition to it, from the person of the Messenger ﷺ.

We observe the rumour coming suddenly to the ears of the Prophet ﷺ, to his human side, wherein he acts, ponders, and contemplates much like any other human. He became agitated like others became agitated, questioned like others question, considered things by their merits, and consulted those knowledgeable from his companions.

It is from the fittingness of Divine Wisdom, in clarifying this human aspect within the Prophet ﷺ, that revelation was delayed to the extent it was so that people could witness two realities in his person, both being the utmost of importance.

As for the first reality, it is that the Prophet ﷺ did not part from being human by means of prophethood and his mission. Hence, it is not proper for the one who believes in him to imagine that prophethood surpasses the limits of mankind and to ascribe to him ﷺ what shouldn't be ascribed, except to Allah ﷻ alone.

As for the second reality, it is that Divine Revelation was not the personal intuitions, ideas or thoughts emerging from the person of Muhammad ﷺ, just as it was not a thing subjected to his will, aspirations, or desires. If that was the case, it would have been easy for him – rather, demanded from himself – to end this rumour from the first day it arose, to relieve himself from its consequences. He would have moulded the Qur'an with what he believed of the goodness and righteousness of his family. Thereby, putting the hearts of his believing companions at ease and silencing intruding meddlers. Yet he did nothing of the sort, preferring to silently suffer with the resulting uneasiness and bubbling of doubt. Since the Qur'an was not his to own.

Dr Muhammad Abdullah Darraz mentions in his book, *'Al-Naba' Al-Adheem'*, clarifying this important point:

"Did not the hypocrites spread the slander against his wife, Sayidah A'isha ﷺ, with revelation being delayed and the matter elongated until it reached breaking point and all he ﷺ could say was – I know nothing of her except goodness – with complete self-control and caution? Then, after exhausting all means of investigation, enquiry, and consultation with his companions, and after a complete month had passed, and after all those who knew her were asked, he would say – We don't know of any evil in her. The most he said to her, at the last moment was – O A'isha. Such and such news about you has reached me. If you are innocent, Allah will exonerate you and if you have committed a sin, seek Allah's Forgiveness.

This was all he spoke, from the intuition of his heart. It was like the speech of other men, not knowing the Unseen – but a sincere man, who doesn't allow conjecture to overrule him, nor does he speak of that which he has no knowledge of. And before he could rise from his place after saying these words, those verses from Surah Al-Nur were revealed announcing her innocence and were an irrefutable judgement of her nobility and purity.

If the matter of the Qur'an was in his hands, what stopped him from fabricating verses to protect his honour, defend his home and by ascribing it to heavenly revelation, silence the tongues of the false accusers? Yet never did he spread a lie amongst people or tell a lie on behalf of God – **And had he ascribed to Us even a (single) fabricated thing, We would have seized him with full force and might[31]."**

I put forth that Sayidah A'isha ﷺ, was the first to present these two realities, so that she directed her belief and worship to Allah ﷻ alone, forgetting all besides, and other than Him. Hence, she replied to her mother when she requested her to stand and thank the Messenger of Allah ﷺ, 'I will not stand for him nor thank anyone except Allah ﷻ, for He has declared my innocence.'

These words may appear to somewhat lack the proper etiquette towards the Messenger ﷺ. But the circumstance and condition drove her to those words, a situation weaved by Divine Wisdom, reinforcing

---

31 Quran, Surah Al-Haaqah, (69:45-46).

the creed of the Muslim, severing the slanders of the hypocrites and disbelievers, and clarifying the meaning of Tawheed and proper servitude to Allah ﷻ.

So, this is the significance of the Qur'an's exoneration of Sayidah A'isha ﷺ from this false accusation. This situation, which the Messenger ﷺ endured for an entire month, verified two truths.

Firstly, that the Qur'an was not the work of Muhammad ﷺ, it was not a body of lies spoken against the Name of Allah.

Secondly, the Prophet Muhammad ﷺ, was of the highest standard of trustworthiness towards the revelation of Allah. Never did he add a letter, nor did he ever discard one. If there ever was a pressing and dire need to do so, it would have been this suffocating moment that would have pushed him to it. Truly, he chose to suffer in that difficult, suffocating misfortune through and through, rather than fabricate a lie upon the name of Allah ﷻ. We certainly have evidence from his patience, that if revelation had remained silent on uncovering the truth of this matter, the Messenger ﷺ would have continued to remain upon his patience. And he would not fabricate a lie against Allah, but only deal with the matter with his own human capabilities and judgements.

Moving on, the Quranic judgement that says, **'Truly those who brought forth the lie were a group among you. Do not suppose it to be an evil for you.**

Rather, it is a good for you. Unto each among them is the sin they committed. And he among them who undertook the greater part of it, his shall be a terrible torment.' – is the Decree of Allah and His Words. It doesn't contain any human input from Muhammad ﷺ or anyone else in its meanings or wording. And God forbid that His Words contain any discrepancy or falsehood.

And look at the linguistical precision, reaching the limits of perfection, in revealing the falsehood of this slander. How it expresses that even its original advocate knew of its being a lie, knowing with all certainty that what he was embroiling himself in and spreading in slander, had no foundation to it.

The Testimony of Allah ﷻ came with declaration that this accusation was fabricated from its very roots, by the very first sentence of this Divine Proclamation. The reader stops at the fact that Allah ﷻ testifies of it being a slander and fabrication, before completing the first sentence. And that is when the rumour is introduced as 'the lie'. The word used (in Arabic '*ifk*'), is the worst type of lie and for slandering another, in which the liar knows himself as a liar and fabricator. So, when you begin reading the first part of this verse and reach the word 'lie' ('*ifk*'), you have understood the judgment of Allah ﷻ in regard to this matter, before even completing the sentence, yet alone what comes after it.

The Heirs of Ibn Sulool

We have learnt about Ibn Sulool and his spite that drove him towards promoting a chain of intrigues, the slander being most grave and serious. His intentions were not hidden from the people of Medina to the extent that even his supporters dispersed from his side and methods.

The question whose answer is not hidden from any intelligent person is – was Ibn Sulool the first and last to bear such hostility and engross himself in such purposes?

If this was the case of Ibn Sulool, when he saw the Messenger ﷺ, his evidences of prophethood and truthfulness and even outwardly professed Islam and all that didn't stop him from fabricating such a vicious slander between the ranks of the early Muslims, what then is the case of those in our own times? Such as Christian extremists whose enmity has ripened in the wine-jug of long centuries? Or the harm of Zionism as it has spread and become established? Or from the pens of Western Colonialism or Eastern Marxism[32] against hearts and minds? What of them when they come across the inheritance of Ibn Sulool?

Indeed, the purposes of Ibn Sulool are one and the same of every pointless person persisting on the point of the slander until our point in time. Look at the

---

[32] Perhaps the political side of Marxism has waned and disappeared, yet its philosophical side continues to influence social life.

aim Ibn Sulool harboured, which he became known for and which was not hidden from anyone around him. Know that it is the same aim which the heirs of Ibn Sulool harbour in their hearts in this age.

Finally, the two points to consider below rationally put an end to any insistence on the matter of the slander.

Firstly, is the Qur'an a fabrication from Muhammad ﷺ and a body of lies against Allah ﷻ? If so, then Ibn Sulool had a right to uphold all his purposes and insinuations. It would mean that Muhammad ﷺ, despite everything he displayed of proofs, truthfulness and trustworthiness was, God forbid, a liar and fabricator.

Or is the Qur'an, the Speech of Allah, sent down upon Muhammad ﷺ? With Muhammad ﷺ having no role other than transmitting it with all impartiality and sincerity? In which case, Sayidah A'isha ؓ is innocent from what she was accused of by the testimony of God ﷻ. And Ibn Sulool was the one immersed in lies and slander against Allah ﷻ. This is to be considered before all else.

How ridiculous that you find a man truthful in his claim of faith in Allah ﷻ, his Books and his Messengers, and then picks up the dregs of doubt like that insinuated by Ibn Sulool! How ridiculous to think a man can have even an atom of faith, who insists on any doubt against the honour of Sayidah A'isha ؓ, after considering all that has been mentioned, and when the one who says – **'Truly those who brought forth the lie were a group among you.'** – is Allah ﷻ, Himself!

***

Ali ﷺ and the Event of the Slander

I have not found in the works of the trustworthy historians, biographers nor the scholars of *'ilm al-rijal'* (the science of deducing the reliability of narrators), any allegation that the stance of Ali ﷺ at the event of the slander caused any resentment to A'isha ﷺ and that it further settled in her heart till her last days.

Yet, we come across what modern-day writers repeat and publish. Those who are absorbed with a psychoanalytical approach to history, its events and personalities. First put forth by Sigmund Freud, those impressed by him used his ideas in a way to achieve their purposes through the inquiry of history. In a manner that appeals and agrees to their whims and serves their agendas. I say, that when we listen to such people, we find new opinions that have no precedent in what the reliable, early scholars and historians have put forth. Especially among what the most distinguished have said on this matter, those with the greatest right to speak, the scholars of *ilm al-rijal*.

What I know is that using this modern method of psychoanalysis in the analysis of historical events, trying to analyse the psyches of its people and heroes, is a new art through which some writers wish to appear as clever, hoping to be described with the skill of their analysis of people and their hidden intentions. Yet others would use it as a means to actualise their agendas, by the fanning of plots, sowing of lies or fabricating of truths.

Some of these writers, and I don't know from which of the aforementioned groups they are, have written about Ali:
'Despite his knowledge of her innocence, he took a harsh stance against her, in which he expressed most clearly his own perceptions against her. A'isha had every right to not forget this gesture that almost destroyed her very soul – if not that Allah had shown His Kindness on His Messenger and her by sending down the declaration of her innocence to be recited in the Qur'an till the Day of Judgement.'[33]

The stance of Ali which the writer is referring to, is when the Messenger consulted some of his Companions about separating from A'isha to which Ali suggested, 'Allah has not made things difficult upon you and women are many (for you to marry). And ask the slave-girl she will tell you the truth.'

If we were to have an inclination for the precepts of psychoanalysis in understanding the psyche and

---

[33] Perhaps it is best to not mention the name of this book and its writer. We believe he has now abandoned this view. And he certainly has virtues that make him worthy of being rid of this fantasy and returning to reality.

identifying the reasons behind the words of Ali ﷺ, we do not find – and this is the plain truth – any hint of allegation or any expression of anger. Just like we do not find any sign of a grudge or enmity spilling out from A'isha ﷺ and dominating her behaviour towards him.

The Messenger ﷺ did not consult those from his Companions he did, so that they could speak their minds on whether she was really involved in the matter or whether she was innocent. He knew of the righteousness of his wife and her goodness and steadfastness better than anyone else. Neither would the Prophet ﷺ think to put them in a situation in which they had no legal standing in Islamic law to speak about (that is affirming the accusation). If any of them did speak so, it would have warranted the Islamic legal punishment – the same that befell Hassan ibn Thabit and the others. So how can it be thought that the Prophet ﷺ would put them in a position to speak and then have them whipped for it afterwards?

The Prophet ﷺ only consulted them to put an end to the disorder surrounding him due to the harm of the man who spread evil words against his family, its harm touching the most private of his affairs. And so, he questioned on the minbar all his people asking to be relieved from the pain he was afflicted with because of this evil allegation. It had wounded him most severely with just a few words that had fastened themselves to his family.

Ali ﷺ certainly understood this context of the Prophet's ﷺ question. It was perfectly natural in order to see the Prophet ﷺ, whom he cared and loved so much, to be relieved from his pain that Ali ﷺ replied in the manner he did. His words did not insinuate anything against A'isha ﷺ, rather it was an appeal to the Messenger ﷺ that he not suffer from this matter any longer. He said these words not with the accusation itself in mind. He said them in the sense that if it was his marriage causing him such distress and disturbance, then the Prophet ﷺ did have the option to possibly marry other women.

And certainly, A'isha ﷺ did not discern any other meaning from Ali's words but this. Everything she suffered from agony and suffocation was parted with and dispelled the moment Divine Revelation declared her innocent and the whole incident labelled as 'the lie'. No one ever heard her, May Allah's Pleasure be upon her, blame Ali ﷺ or say anything harsh against him, let alone anything less than that.

As for the Battle of Jamel, which followed the assassination of Uthman ﷺ, it has no relevance whatsoever to our topic here. Extrapolation on that incident will come in a later chapter, Allah willing.

Let us ask, as Professor Abdul Hameed Tahmaaz does in his book *Al-Sayidah A'isha* – which of the two was greater in their effect on Sayidah A'isha. The words of Hassan ibn Thabit ﷺ, who (spread the rumour) and was punished for it, or the words of

Ali ﷺ, whose words, as we saw, contain no blemish of accusation?

The Professor mentions:

'The Lady ﷺ did not show any grudge against Hassan. Rather, her magnanimity carried her to a position of forgiveness towards him. To the extent she would forbid people from cursing him or causing him any injury. In Sahih Bukhari, on the authority of Urwa ﷺ who said, "I began to curse Hassan ibn Thabit next to A'isha. She said: Do not curse him. For he would defend the Messenger of Allah ﷺ.

As for Abdul Razzak, he brings another narration on the authority of Ma'mar who narrates from Qatada, "A'isha would say: Do not say anything about Hassan except goodness. For his poetry would defend the Prophet ﷺ and scoff at the polytheists." He also mentions, "When Hassan would visit A'isha, she would throw out a cushion for him and he would sit on it." Is it to be supposed that the Lady ﷺ would respect Hassan's support for the Prophet ﷺ and forgive his extreme offence and injury against her, but not respect the many more stances of Ali ﷺ in support of the Prophet ﷺ, his courage in battle and many sacrifices in the path of Islam!?' [34]

I add on that such would be the case if they were on equal footing (regarding accusing). Then what is the case when when Ali ﷺ never mentioned any accusation and he didn't intend except to lighten the burden upon the Messenger of Allah ﷺ?

---
34 As-Sayidah A'isha, Abdul Hameed Tahmaaz. Pg, 145.

We have searched and investigated yet could find no trace of any stance or words that indicated A'isha holding any grudge against Ali because of his aforementioned words. In fact, we notice that most of the hadith that praise the virtues of Ali and Fatima were in fact narrated by A'isha.

From the reliable narrations, A'isha was asked, 'Who was the most beloved to the Messenger of Allah?'

She replied, 'Fatima.'

It was then asked, 'And from the men?'

She replied, 'Her husband (i.e., Ali). He was, as you know, perpetually fasting the days and praying the nights.'[35]

It was also she, who narrated the hadith of the virtues of the *Ahl ul-Bait* (Family of the Prophet), considered one of the greatest virtues of Ali, may Allah's Pleasure be upon him. She narrates, 'The Prophet left early one morning and over him was a black, woollen cloak. Al-Hassan came to him and the Prophet entered him under the cloak. Then came Al-Hussein and entered with him. Then along came Fatima and he made her enter too. Then came Ali, who the Prophet also covered. The Prophet then recited, '**Allah only intends to remove all the impurity of sins from you, O People**

---

35 Narration of Tirmidhi

of the House (of the Prophet) and purify to the utmost purity.'[36]

***

The Spiteful and their Flawed Interpretations

However, what is worse than the schemes of Christian Fundamentalists or other religious groups, are the repugnant interpretations of those who absolve themselves of logic and deny the rules of Arabic grammar and hold maliciousness towards the wives of the Messenger of Allah ﷺ. Yet people imagine them as the lovers of the Prophet's Family!

One of them has said:
'It has only been made apparent from the ten Quranic verses on the innocence of A'isha, that the Words of Allah – **Why did they not produce four witnesses? For when they brought not the witnesses, it is they who were then liars in the sight of Allah** – *imply their lying was because of their absence of bringing forth witnesses. It is obvious that not bringing about witnesses is only a sign of apparent innocence. It is a legal judgement of innocence without true innocence, it reveals the absence of a link between the two'!*[37]

Any intelligent person who can free himself of hatred against the wives of the Messenger of

---

36 Narration of Muslim.
37 Al- Mizan fi Tafsir al Quran. Sayyid Muhammad Hussain Al- Tabatabai

Allah ﷻ and his purified family (*Ahl ul-Bait*), must undoubtedly wonder when he hears this abominable ploy. Are we to believe that the concern and worry which was keeping the Prophet ﷺ awake from sleep and was so occupying his mind, was suddenly relieved, the happiness to his face magically returned and made him reunite lovingly with his wife, only because she was legally exonerated, despite some hidden reality that could be to the contrary!?

If the matter was as they claim (which no intelligent person can accept), then why did the Prophet ﷺ allow such distress and sorrow to affect him at the beginning of the incident? Since he already knew – even before revelation of the verses of innocence and as necessitated by the Shariah punishment for defamation which had already been revealed – that Sayidah A'isha ؓ was never in threat of receiving legal punishment anyway. Since no one witnessed any immorality from her, let alone the four witnesses required by Shariah Law for the legal punishment to be binding!

Indeed, the worry that he was overtaken with, which was observable by one and all, was his concern that the rumour spread throughout Medina was true in its reality, regardless of the presence or absence of witnesses, that is, regardless of the absence of evidence for the Shariah ruling.

So, when he was freed from the ordeal and the

verses came down exonerating Sayidah A'isha ﷺ and incriminating the group with the crime of slander and defamation, cheer and brightness returned to the face of the Messenger ﷺ. This itself was absolute evidence that those verses contained within them the meanings of actual innocence as well as the *Shari*, legal innocence. It made clear her actual innocence when it revealed the truth, when it brought happiness into the heart of the Messenger of Allah ﷺ and highlighted Sayidah A'isha's ﷺ elevation far and above what the slanderers tried to bind her with. And then, it made clear her legal exoneration by applying the *Shari* judgement (i.e., whipping) upon the slanderers and spreaders.

Look at the first sentence from these ten (Qur'anic) verses. You will notice that the words spread by the slandering group was not called except by one description – 'the lie' (in Arabic *ifk*). And *ifk* is the worst type of lying in Arabic. The speaker of such a lie would not be named so, except if he knew full he was lying in what he insinuated. It is a Divine declaration of Sayidah A'isha's ﷺ innocence from what was alleged and at the same time it labelled the accusation as a lie and fabrication.

As for one who witnesses someone committing adultery and his testimony is rejected because it is not reinforced by at least three others, then such testimony is not labelled as a lie and does not attract the punishment of lying per se. As he is truthful in what he witnessed and informed of – if it is supposed he is being honest. Yet he is still to be punished the whipping of bringing about a slander as he has removed the veil on what Allah ﷻ had left drawn. This is what is meant by the Shari, legal exoneration acquired because of the veiling of Allah ﷻ.

Look at these slanderers, how they play with the Words of Allah to subdue them to their grudges and their own selves' desires. When in the first sentence of this clear, Divine Speech, which describes the claim of the group in question as 'the lie', tears apart this petty, maligning interpretation.

I have not read anything in defence of the lie of Ibn Ubay, which undermines the truth settled by the Book of Allah ﷻ, in such a shameful, concealing manner like this strange, contradictory statement which you have read!

He defends Ibn Ubay and his party in what they spread and alleged, only because he denies the true innocence, but does not deny the *Shari*/legal innocence which is the field of inquiry…and because there is no concordance between the actual innocence and the legal innocence, as he says, then it is the right of Ibn Ubay to accuse her and rob her of her innocence in regards to the reality of the matter and leave for her only the innocence which the law veils her with…and then (he claims) the description in the Quran of Ibn Ubay and his party as liars is out of the question!

And still it remains, (for their claim to be valid)

that the Messenger ﷺ also understood the matter this way. But such thoughts were absent from his mind and understanding. If he did understand it according to their way, he would have resigned himself to more worry and grief and expose himself to more wearying doubt towards his wife, who somehow was vindicated by the law but actually guilty!

They do not impose upon the Messenger ﷺ anything less than to ignore and disregard the words of Allah – **"Truly those who brought forth the lie..."** – and instead believe and yield to the words of Ibn Ubay, who exonerated A'isha ؓ legally but not in reality!!!

You may consider orientalists, like Schacht, Goldziher and Bernard Lewis and wonder if they have also become disciples of this school of lowly slander with this fabrication against Allah ﷻ, His Messenger ﷺ and renunciation of basic logic with such statements!

SAYIDAH A'ISHA'S SCHOLARLY PROMINENCE

What there is no disagreement in between the historians and biographers, is that the Companions ﷺ, whenever they were faced with a difficult matter of religion, in which they were unable to find a solution to, would refer to Sayidah A'isha ﷺ and find the answer which had alluded them of knowledge.

Zarkasha narrates in the book, *Al-Ijabah*, on the authority of Abu Musa Al-Ashari ﷺ, "Never did a hadith cause ambiguity to us, the Companions of the Messenger of Allah ﷺ, except that we would refer it to A'isha and find her having knowledge of it.'

While Ibn Hajar ﷺ narrates in his book, *Al-Isaabah*, that Masrooq, one of the tabieen says, 'I saw the great of the Companions of the Messenger of Allah ﷺ asking A'isha ﷺ about the obligatory actions (of worship)'.

It has been narrated by Ata' ibn Abi Ribah, 'A'isha was among the most knowledgeable of people and most excellent in her opinion.' Hisham bin Urwa mentions from his father, 'I haven't seen anyone more knowledgeable in fiqh nor medicine nor poetry than A'isha.' Al-Zuhri says, 'If the knowledge of A'isha was gathered on the one side and on the other side were the rest of the Mothers of the Believers and women companions, the knowledge of A'isha would have outshone them.'[38]

Zarkashi authored a book he titled *Al-Ijaabah fi ma Istadrakathu A'isha ala al-Sahabah* (*A'isha's responses in correcting the Companions*) in which he gathers some corrections Sayidah A'isha made to the understandings or narrations of some of the Companions.

Even though much of what Zarkashi transmits has not been verified as authentic in terms of its *sanad* (chain of narration), the corrections Sayidah A'isha made to the Companions, mostly in the proper transmission of hadith and sometimes in their understandings of them, cannot be denied. At times her difference with them was only her opinion or difference in *ijtihad* (scholarly deduction) and so not binding on the Companion in question to change his opinion for hers. But disagreement of the Companions with her in terms of the proper transmission of a hadith was extremely rare.

Amongst the critiques of Sayidah A'isha that have been recorded as evidence of her unique methodology and that differed to that of many of the Companions, foremost Abdullah ibn Abbas, was the matter of the Messenger seeing his Lord on the Night of Ascension (*Mi'raj*). Narrated by Bukhari and others, Masrooq relates, 'I asked A'isha, "O Mother, did Muhammad see his Lord?"

---

[38] Isaabah, Al-Hafiz ibn Hajar

She replied, "You have made my hairs stand on their ends from what you have asked! Where are you regarding three (Qur'anic verses), whoever contradicts them has lied. (First) Whoever says to you that Muhammad ﷺ saw his Lord has lied." – And she recited the Words of Allah – "**Eyes cannot grasp Him, He grasps sight itself! Yet He is Most Kind, Most Well Informed**"[39] and "**It is not for man that he speaks to Allah except through revelation or from behind a veil.**"[40]

(She continued) "And whoever says to you that he knows what tomorrow will bring, then he has lied" – and she recited Allah's Words – "**Indeed, it is only Allah who has knowledge of the Hour. He sends down (knowledge of) the Unseen and knows what is concealed in the womb. No soul knows what it will earn the morrow.**"[41]

"And whoever says that the Messenger held something back (i.e., not informed the people about regarding religion) then he has lied." – And she recited the Words of Allah – "**O Messenger, convey (all) which has been revealed upon you**"[42]. However, he did see Angel Jibril ﷺ in his actual form twice.'"[43]

The two shaykhs also narrate from Ziyaad ibn Abi Sufyaan who wrote a letter to Sayidah

---

39 Quran, Surah Anaam, (6:103).
40 Quran, Surah Shuraa, (42:51).
41 Quran, Surah Luqmaan, (31:34).
42 Quran, Surah Ma'idah, (5:67).
43 Sahih Bukhari, Kitab al-Tawheed.

A'isha ؓ saying: Abdullah ibn Abbas has said that whoever brought an animal for sacrifice, the same is forbidden on him as is forbidden on the Hajj pilgrim until the animal is sacrificed. And I have brought my animal for sacrifice. Write back to me your advice.

She wrote back to him saying: It is not as Ibn Abbas has said. I plaited the rope to bind the animal of the Messenger of Allah ﷺ with my own hands. Then the Messenger ﷺ roped it (around the animal) with his own hands. Then he sent it along with my father. And yet it was not made forbidden on him (what is made forbidden on the Hajj pilgrim) until the animal was sacrificed.[44]

There is also the matter of Abu Huraira ؓ holding an opinion on account of Abdullah ibn Abbas ؓ and changing it on hearing Sayidah A'isha's correction. He initially held the opinion that the one who reaches the time of *fajr* (pre-dawn) in a state of *junoob* (greater ritual impurity), cannot fast on that day. However, when Sayidah A'isha ؓ and Umm Salamah ؓ were both asked, they said that the Messenger ﷺ would wake up in a state of *junoob*, from other than a nocturnal emission, and he would still fast. When Abu Huraira ؓ was informed, he said, 'They are more knowledgeable (of the matter)' and changed his position regarding it.

She also corrected Abdullah ibn Umar ؓ when it reached her that he was saying

---

44 Agreed upon hadith.

that the dead are punished in their graves by the weeping of the living – or the weeping of their family. It is a hadith narrated by the two shaykhs.

She said, 'May Allah forgive Abi Abdul Rahman (Abdullah ibn Umar). He would not lie, but he has forgotten or made a mistake. The Messenger ﷺ passed by a Jewish woman who was crying over the death of one of her relatives. The words of the Messenger of Allah ﷺ were only specific to that dead man. He was pointing to the fact that the crying of one's relative doesn't benefit one after leaving this world as a disbeliever. Rather crying over him only increases him in regret and sorrow.' She then recited the Words of Allah that reject taking the hadith in a general sense, '**None bears the burdens of another.**'[45]

The scholars have had long discourse, with much debate, on the meaning intended by the Messenger of Allah ﷺ when he said, "The deceased is certainly punished by the crying of his family over him." In some narrations of Bukhari, the hadith appears as '*some of* the crying of his family'. Such disagreement is even after Sayidah A'isha ﷺ attempted to explain it by differentiating between its general or specific application and in accordance with the words of Allah ﷻ, '**None bears the burdens of another.**'

Perhaps what best reconciliates between the hadith and the verse is that the word 'punished' in the hadith refers to the feelings of distress because of his

---
45 Quran, Surah Anaam, (6:164).

knowledge of his family crying over him, not because of the punishment of the angels as the hadith gives the illusion. It means that the deceased is further agitated and drained because of his family's crying over him, especially if it entails wailing and howling. He wishes they would not do so.[46]

Moving on, at times the Companions differed amongst themselves in the meaning of a hadith or its narration and would refer it Sayidah A'isha, agreeing wholeheartedly and being contented with her opinion or decision.

From amongst which is the hadith of Abu Huraira in the books of Bukhari and Muslim, 'Whoever follows a funeral procession has a *Qiraat* (a mountain of rewards).' Ibn Umar on hearing him say that commented, 'Abu Huraira must have exaggerated the matter.' He then set out to question Sayidah A'isha and she confirmed that the Messenger of Allah had indeed said that. To which Ibn Umar sighed, 'We have missed out on many a *Qiraat* (mountain of reward).'[47]

Imam Ahmed narrates in his *Musnad* that two men went to question Sayidah A'isha saying, "Abu Huraira says that the Messenger used to say: The bad omen is in women, livestock and the home." On hearing this, Sayidah A'isha's anger reached as if to the heavens and she exclaimed, 'I swear by the One

---

46 Hadith is narrated by Bukhari and Muslim.
47 Bukhari & Muslim. In their Chapters on Funerals.

who sent down the Qur'an to Muhammad, he would never say such a thing. Rather the Prophet of Allah ﷺ would say: *The people at the time of ignorance (Jahiliya) would say* there is a bad omen in women, livestock and the home.' She then recited the words of Allah – "**No calamity occurs in the earth nor in your lives, but it is in a Book before We bring it forth. Surely, that is easy for Allah.**"[48]

In some narrations it was added that she said, 'Abu Huraira did not memorise it correctly, he heard the end of the hadith but not the beginning of it.'

Also narrated by Imam Ahmad ﷺ in his *Musnad* and Al-Hakim ﷺ in his *Mustadarak* is the hadith of Hisham ibn Urwa ﷺ who mentions, Urwa (A'isha's nephew) would say to A'isha, 'O Mother, I am not amazed at your deep knowledge, I say she is the wife of the Messenger of Allah ﷺ and daughter of Abu Bakr ﷺ. Nor am I amazed at your knowledge of poetry and culture for I say she is the daughter of Abu Bakr ﷺ and he was the most knowledgeable in them. However what amazes me is your knowledge of medicine! How and from where did it come to be?

She hit him across the shoulder and said, 'O little Urwa. The Messenger of Allah ﷺ became sick near the end of his life. Delegations from the different Arab tribes came to him, describing different means of treatment and I would treat him. It was from there.'[49]

---

48 Quran, Surah Hadid, (57:22).
49 Musnad Ahmed (76/6), Al Mustadarak (11/4).

Al-Hakim also narrates in his *Mustadarak* that Al-Zuhri said, "If the knowledge of the people was gathered and that of the wives of the Prophet ﷺ, the knowledge of A'isha would be more comprehensive."

But perhaps the choicest of words that describe her knowledge are those penned down by Professor Saeed Al-Afghani in his introduction to Zarkashi's work on A'isha's corrections of the Companions. He says:

"I spent years in the study of Sayidah A'isha, a time that I spent in constant disbelief and amazement which no pen can describe. The most exceptional of what I can mention and what would astonish you, was her rich knowledge which was like a deep ocean with crashing waves, far horizons and shades of colours. You can take from it her mastery of fiqh, or hadith, or tafseer, knowledge of the Shariah, literature, poetry, knowledge of reports, Arab genealogy and their great epics, or medicine, or history. You would find from that what would delight your mind. Nor will your amazement cease knowing that, she achieved all that and still had not surpassed eighteen years of age!"

HER SHARE OF ELOQUENCE AND SKILL OF EXPRESSION

All biographies of Sayidah A'isha are in agreement that she was the most eloquent of Arab women in her time.

Tirmidhi narrates from Musa ibn Talhah, 'I have not seen anyone more eloquent than A'isha'. Muhammad ibn Sireen narrates from Ahnaf ibn Qais, 'I heard the sermon of Abu Bakr as As-Sideeq, Umar ibn Al-Khattab, Uthman ibn Affan, Ali ibn Abi Talib, and the Caliphs till our current day. I have not heard words from any creation more splendid and eloquent than those of A'isha.'[50]

Better than listing down what was said about her eloquence, is that we listen to her directly.

When Abu Bakr passed away, Sayidah A'isha stood by his grave and pronounced, '*May Allah illuminate your face, dear father and reward you for your righteous efforts. For you humiliated the world by turning your back to it. And you honoured the Hereafter when you turned to face it. Indeed, the most momentous event after the passing of the Messenger of Allah, is your passing. The biggest calamity after him, is losing you. The book of Allah promises a good reward for virtuous patience for you. And I seek the promise of Allah through*

---
50 Hakim, Mustadarak.

you with patience. And I will pass it by seeking Allah's Mercy upon you. If they stood for this world, you stood for religion when its people weakened, its cracks stretched, and it shook frantically. Upon you be the peace of Allah. Farewell, without a word spoken in objection against your life. Without a criticism against your judgement."

And from her most eloquent discourses is what she replied to Imran ibn Hussein and Abu Hasan Al-Duali on the day of (the battle) al-Jamal. They asked her, 'O Mother of the Believers. Inform us of your intentions. Is (your setting out with an army) an instruction from the Messenger of Allah ﷺ or your own opinion?'

She replied, '*No, rather it is my opinion that I saw apt when Uthman was killed. Indeed, we have risen to avenge him with the crack of a whip at Sahabatul Muhmaah…for you transgressed over him violating three sanctities that were forbidden: the sanctity of the land (of Medina), the sanctity of the (position of) caliphate and the sanctity of the holy month. He was washed like a bowl[51] and purified. And these oppressors from amongst you executed him. We used to get angry for your sake against Uthman's whip. Shall we not be outraged for Uthman's sake against your sword!?"*[52]

Then there is what she announced on the day Uthman was killed, may Allah be pleased with him.

---

51 That is, Uthman (r) was blamed for some of his judgements and when he changed them, being purified through that gesture, like a bowl is purified after washing it, and hence giving you what you wanted, you transgressed against him and killed him.
52 Al Bidaaya wa Nihaaya ibn Kathir: 7/232.

She asked, '*Has the Commander of the Believers been killed?*'

They replied, 'Yes'.

She continued, '*Allah have mercy on him and forgive him. By Allah, you were in greater need yourselves of establishing the truth, supporting, strengthening, and affirming Islam, rather than in rushing obediently towards the one who was opposed to it. Yet every time Allah increased you in blessings in your religion, you increased in burden to support Him, favouring instead to gain this world. By Allah, the destruction of a blessing is easier than building it up. And increased blessings through gratitude are more difficult to gain than the passing of blessings due to ingratitude.*'

A'ISHA AND WOMEN

As historians agree, Sayidah A'isha ﷺ was a sanctuary for poor and vulnerable women. They would seek refuge in her for the protection and defence of their rights. On occasion, a woman or young girl would be uncomfortable disclosing her grievance directly to the Messenger ﷺ so they would come to A'isha ﷺ, who would act as an intermediary to him. Or she would encourage that the grievance be directly disclosed to the Messenger ﷺ.

An-Nisai narrates that A'isha ﷺ mentioned that a young girl visited her and said, 'My father has married me to his brother's son so that he might raise his status thereby and I am averse to it.'

A'isha replied, 'Sit down here until the Messenger of Allah arrives.'

When the Messenger arrived, I informed him. He sent word to her father, calling him, and he left the choice of the matter in her hands. She said, 'O Messenger of Allah, I accept what my father did, but I wanted to make it known to women that fathers don't have final authority in the matter.'

There were also some men at the time, who would continuously oppress their wives by divorcing them, until when their *iddah*[53] was almost completed, they would take them back, only to divorce them again. So, she remained due to that, neither married nor free to remarry. Tirmidhi narrates from A'isha ﷺ, "The people were such that a man would divorce his wife when he wanted to divorce her, and if he wanted, he could take her back during her *iddah*. He could divorce her a hundred times or even more to the extent he would say, 'I will not divorce you that you be free of me, nor keep you with me.'

She would say, 'And how is that?'

He would say, 'I will divorce you and whenever your *Iddah* is just about to end I will take you back'."

So, a woman went to A'isha ﷺ to inform her about that and A'isha ﷺ was silent and delayed the woman until the Messenger of Allah ﷺ arrived. She informed him of the matter and the Prophet ﷺ was also silent, till Allah revealed the Quranic verse: '**Divorce is but twice. Then is holding on to her with kindness or setting her free with goodness.**'[54] A'isha ﷺ said, "The people then carried on with divorce, (knowing) who was divorced and who was not."

She, may Allah's Pleasure be upon her, would denounce anything that belittled the dignity of women. She once heard someone narrating that the prayer is not broken except by a dog, donkey, or woman (i.e.,

---

[53] A period of 3 months for divorced women in which they can't remarry and the husband can re-establish the marriage.
[54] Quran; Surah Baqarah, (2:229)

if they were to pass in front of one while praying it would break one's prayer). She became angry and vocal in her condemnation saying, 'You compare us to donkeys and dogs? The Messenger of Allah ﷺ would pray in the night and my leg would fall in front of him or by his side and he would move it aside and I would pull it away (and the Prophet would continue praying).'[55]

While the two shaykhs narrate that when the above narration was mentioned to her – that prayer is nullified by the donkey, dog, and woman – she said, 'You have compared us to donkeys and dogs! By Allah, I saw the Messenger of Allah ﷺ praying and I was laying on the mattress between him and the *qibla*. Then I required to visit the latrine and I hated to disturb the Messenger ﷺ by sitting up, so I slipped out from the edge of the bed.'[56]

And we have mentioned her condemning Abu Huraira's narration of the hadith, "The bad omen is only in women, the livestock and the home.' To which she replied, 'I swear by the One who sent down the Qu'ran on Abu Qasim (Muhammad) ﷺ, he never said it as such. Rather the Messenger of Allah ﷺ would say, *'The people of Jahiliya would say* the bad omen is in women, the livestock and the home.'

And even if she had not defended the status of women and their rights with such stances, then the

---
[55] Al-Ijaabah, Zarkashi. Tahqeeq Ustaz Saeed Al-Afghani, p 125.
[56] Bukhari.

life that this Lady built was – as Professor Saeed Al-Afghani says – *'soaring glory for the academic tradition of women in Islam. Rather, her genius alone suffices to fill an entire history. We do not know of the genius of any man or woman in the history of nations that came close to the station of this Lady. And all Muslim ladies should know that at the beginning of Islam, there was one of you, who taught the great from the Companions of the Ansar and Muhajireen, each intellectual, each scholar, faqih and narrator from them. And from her alone, is transmitted a quarter of the Shariah as Al-Hakim mentionin his Mustadarak.'*[57]

---

57 Foreword to Al-Ijaabah. Ustaz Saeed Al-Afghani. Pg. 6.

THE WORSHIP OF A'ISHA, HER PIETY & ABSTINENCE

Sayidah A'isha was one who would fast profusely, until one would think that she was always in a fasting state. Likewise, she was diligent in praying deep into the night. She would beseech Allah with profound humility in prayer. And if she passed by a verse that invoked fear or carried a threat, she would repeat it, entreating Allah with what suited the context of the verse.

Al-Hafiz Abu Naeem narrates in *Al-Hilya*, from Abu Dhuha who said, 'Someone informed me that they heard A'isha recite in her prayer – "**Then Allah blessed us and saved us from the smoking chastisement.**"[58] It made her cry and say, "(O Allah) Bless me...and save me from the smoking chastisement." And the one who heard her recite the verse – "**And stay in your homes**"[59] – informed me that she cried till her veil was soaked. And she would fast and fast until the scorching heat of the day would wither her.'

Once Ibn Munkadir sent her some wealth filling two bags having a value of what was said to be equal to eighty or a hundred thousand dirhams. She called for a plate, and she was fasting that day, sat down and

---
58 Quran; Surah Tur {52:27}
59 Quran; Surah Ahzab {33:33}

began distributing it amongst the poor. By evening, not a single dirham remained. When it became time to break her fast, she called out to her servant girl to bring her something to break her fast and she came with some bread and oil. The servant girl said, 'Could you not spare a single dirham so that we could buy some meat to break our fast with?'

A'isha ﷺ replied, 'Do not be too harsh with me. If you had reminded me, I would have done so.'

Abdul Rahman ibn Qasim narrates that Muawiya ﷺ sent her garments and silverware as well as other things. When A'isha came out and her glance fell on them, she wept and said, 'But the Messenger of Allah never came across such things'. She then distributed it until nothing of it remained.

Abdul Rahman ibn Qasim also narrates, 'I gifted her with baskets of grapes and she distributed them. Her slave girl snatched away a basket without her knowing. When it was night, she brought it forth and A'isha said, 'What is this?'

She replied, 'My master, I kept it back so we could eat from it.'

A'isha replied, 'Would not a single bunch have sufficed? By Allah, I will not eat anything from it.'

Some may think that her abstinence only began after the passing of the Messenger of Allah ﷺ however, it was also her custom during the life of the Messenger ﷺ. Never did any wealth enter upon her person, but she would give it all in charity or the greater portion of it. Sometimes she would seek more of Allah's Bounty by giving a little and He would bless her with greater wealth soon after, only for her to donate that as well.

She narrates, 'A poor woman came to me carrying two daughters with her, so I gave her three dates – and that was all that she had. She fed a date to each child but when she raised the third to her mouth, her daughters reached out towards it. So, she split that date she had intended to eat into two and shared it among them. Her matter amazed me, so I mentioned it later to the Prophet ﷺ. He replied that truly, Allah has made Paradise compulsory on her because of that or that she has been set free from the Fire.'[60]

---

[60] Hilyatul Awliya, 2/49.

A WORD ON THE JEALOUSY BETWEEN THE MOTHERS OF THE BELIEVERS

Some writers are fascinated by the jealously that appeared from time to time between the Mothers of the Believers generally and especially between them and Sayidah A'isha ﷺ. You see such writers collecting reports, at times exaggerating in their depictions, presenting the relationships between the Mothers of the Believers as two competing blocs or factions.

What I clearly see however, is that being involved in such a line of enquiry, focusing on and highlighting the appearances of jealously between the wives of the Prophet ﷺ, is nothing but investigating what is already obvious. It is nothing but turning attention to a characteristic trait that Allah ﷻ has implanted in women – regardless of their differences in virtue or refinement of character. Such discourse, or occupation with the narrations and events that allude to this matter, does not bring about any benefit to the inquirer who records it nor to the reader who seeks enlightenment.

We would do well to keep in mind that feelings of jealousy between women and its expression between women, does not detract from the virtue of women. Nor does it diminish her elevated character any less – as long as those feelings don't push one to perpetrate evil and what is forbidden. And how far it is from imagination, that you would find between A'isha 🙏 and the other Mothers of the Believers, any behaviour that would tarnish their lofty characters, which they were all well known by.

That is one point to be made. Another is that the status which the wives of the Messenger 🕌 occupy, which requires our respect and esteem as well as holding back our pens and tongues from criticising or causing offense to them, is not to say they are infallible or free from error. For there is none who can claim such innocence except the Messengers and Prophets. But our respect is a result of the respect the Messenger of Allah 🕌 showed to them, their attachment to the Messenger 🕌 in the house of prophethood and their companionship in the most exclusive of his affairs and in the vicissitudes of circumstances. No doubt, this is a definite evidence of the great virtue that Allah 🕌 distinguished them with. To then look for their errors or flaws and focus the spotlight on them with defamation and criticism, only highlights the considerable deficiency the investigator suffers from. It would be better for him to rather investigate and evaluate his own self and rectify his inner demons and the reality of his state.

This logical and religious conclusion we have mentioned also applies generally to all the Companions 🙏. About whom the Messenger 🕌 said in an authentic tradition, 'Fear Allah! Fear Allah regarding my companions. Don't take them as targets after me. For whoever has loved them, they have done so out of love for me. And whoever shows enmity towards them, has done so out of enmity to me. And whoever harms them, has harmed me.'[61]

This instruction from the Prophet ﷺ does not mean that his Companions ؓ were free from error or sin. Rather it means, in any case, they hold a position with Allah ﷻ that none that come after them can reach. This necessitates reverence to them and the absence of long tongues of criticism and belittlement.

Criticising speech that is composed of concentrating on the errors of others, uncovering them, making assumptions, conjuring up their faults, and unleashing one's personal foolishness and dogmatic thought upon those errors – has become today a new art with which many writers attempt to show themselves as clever. Whether it be so that eyes may be turned towards them and they may become known after they were inconspicuous, or to water the thirst of their fanaticism, or to delude people to think that they themselves are innocent from such faults with which they criticise others.

Look to the many pens that collect or falsify faults and then scatter them around about Uthman ؓ, or Khalid bin Walid ؓ, or Abu Huraira ؓ, or Muawiya ؓ, or so and so from the Companions, may Allah be pleased with all of them. It is an abominable shamelessness we have not known or seen in the pens of earlier writers and researchers.

---

[61] Narration of Tirmidhi

That is because earlier writers and scholars would be cautious in what they recorded and researched into, so they could be constructive and reformative to society. They knew well that amusement by picking on the flaws of earlier generations, whoever they may be, is not conducive to reforming a society. Rather, it is one of the more dangerous means that lead to corruption and harm.

As for these new writers and criticisers, one of them may only intend – as we have mentioned – to make himself notable through the criticism of others, to be known for his apparent expertise in identifying the errors of others, in analysing the circumstances of societies, and in discovering shortcomings and flaws.

There is no way to remedy an event whose time has passed, it being designated to the repository of history. But he (i.e., the unfair researcher) can build for himself acclaim, not by acquiring virtue, but by sitting upon the debris of the good reputations of men and women, after much destruction and sowing corruption.

Evidence of this is that one of them flings their arrows of criticism back through centuries to those peerless individuals without stopping a single moment to look at himself in the mirror. In which are gathered the same, multiplied defects which he seeks elsewhere. If only he would put himself on the same scale of criticism and treat himself from his many shortcomings – even with just one of those arrows.

We once again repeat, that the presentation of reports to highlight signs of jealously between Sayidah A'isha and the rest of the Mothers of the Believers, does not acquire for us any missing knowledge nor deliver us from blameworthy ignorance. They are facts that, the one who acquires them, is neither elevated through nor decreased, in the areas of virtue, conduct, the *halal* or *haram*.

This jealousy is a feminine nature Allah ﷻ has established in women. And such natural instincts do not submit to any Islamic ruling, nurturing or guidance. Searching for its appearance amongst reports and narrations, is like searching for their tendency for food and drink, rest after effort, or sleep after drowsiness.

DID A'ISHA LEAD AN OPPOSING FACTION?

If there wasn't such striking difference between ingenuity and ineptitude, we might have said that some writers today are just attempting to sound clever by claiming that A'isha ﷺ was leading an opposing faction in the life of the Messenger of Allah ﷺ!

Have you seen anyone who has read or heard from history, the *sirah* or biographies that A'isha ﷺ was quote, '...*an example of strong opposition against the Messenger of Allah ﷺ and his Companions ﷺ at every point of her life...*'?

I certainly have not read such a thing till this day nor have I ever heard such reports about A'isha ﷺ. I know others have also never read or heard anything of the like. Even those who explain the prophethood of Muhammad ﷺ as being a reformative, democratic mission do not claim that his rule consisted of an opposition front.

Yet a journalist tries to appear clever and writes these words that we have never heard of and that eluded those before us for centuries. He emphasises the point that A'isha ﷺ was the strongest individual in opposition to the Messenger ﷺ. And here he is relating to us these negative, opposing stances against him.

Amongst these, he mentions that when the Qur'an was revealed with the order of the Prophet ﷺ marrying Zainab bint Jahsh ؓ after her divorce with Zaid ؓ, A'isha ؓ said, 'I see that your Lord hastens in fulfilling your wishes.'

Another is when the Prophet ﷺ carried his newborn, Ibrahim from Maria Coptiya ؓ, to A'isha ؓ she said, 'I don't see any resemblance between you and him.'

What then is the reality behind these two reports? And where is the evidence of this great opposition in them?

Firstly, Sayidah A'isha ؓ did not say 'I see that your Lord hastens in fulfilling your desires' on Allah's order to marry Zainab ؓ – according to both authentic and weak narrations. If any of the Qur'anic exegetes, hadith scholars, historians or fuqaha had mentioned these words in that context, one might agree with the journalist's claim that the Prophet ﷺ was inclined to marrying Zainab ؓ and that Allah ﷻ was hastening in fulfilling the Prophet's wishes.

In actuality, A'isha ؓ said these words to the Messenger ﷺ on a totally different occasion. There is no evidence to what this writer supposes, near or far.

Imams Bukhari, Muslim, Nisai and Ahmed ibn Hanbal all narrate from A'isha ؓ that she was feeling jealous of the women that were proposing to the Messenger ﷺ. Then when Allah ﷻ revealed the verses, **'…and any believing woman if she gives herself (in marriage) to the Prophet and if the Prophet desires to marry her – for you alone, not for (the rest of) the believers'** until **'It is up to you (O Prophet) to delay or receive whoever you please of your wives. There is no blame on you if you call back any of those you have set aside.'**[62] It was then she said to him, 'I see that your Lord hastens in fulfilling your desires'.

It is known that the Messenger ﷺ did not marry any of the women that proposed to him, yet all the matter was, was that Allah ﷻ allowed it for him, referring the decision to the Prophet's wishes.[63]

So where is the opposing stance or meaning in these words that she said to him? What is even the point of opposition in this situation? The Messenger ﷺ did not marry any woman that proposed to him, so how could A'isha ﷺ even be criticising one of his actions?

Where is even the smell of condemnation in her words in the proper context? Would an Arab not understand from this, except A'isha's wonder at the Messenger's position with his Lord and His great Love for him? And this is how both the scholars and biographers of the Prophet ﷺ understand it.

---

62 Qur'an Surah Ahzab, (33:50-51).
63 See Fath al Bari, 8/733

In fact, this sentence has become famous in the history of the Arabs. It being a most lovely praise that Sayidah A'isha ﷺ formulated out of her amazement with his position with his Lord ﷻ. And it has been repeated in their poetry to praise the Prophet ﷺ. Does it then hide a meaning of opposition or criticism that has been concealed throughout the ages of the Arabs, only being uncovered now by some journalist?

***

As for his second contention, it is what Waqidi narrates from Muhammad ibn Abdullah from Zuhri, from Urwa that A'isha ﷺ said, 'When Ibrahim ﷺ was born, the Messenger ﷺ brought him to me and said, "Look at how he resembles me!"

To which I replied, "I don't see any resemblance..."'

Let us pass over the fact that this narration is weak in its authenticity and ask – Where is the opposition to the Messenger ﷺ in these words? Is it only because A'isha took another opinion on the matter of Ibrahim's likeness to his father?

Have you heard of a family blessed with a child and then its members not differ to whom the child most closely resembles? Does he lean more in likeness to the maternal side or paternal? Does anyone say that such discussion will tear apart the family into opposing factions?

Or perhaps this journalist wants us to understand something more sinister than this typical banter amongst families through the ages? Is it his attempt at slandering Maria ﷺ and accusing her of being treacherous to the Messenger ﷺ, taking the statement that the baby doesn't resemble him as a witness to this?

If this is what he is driving at, then it is an accusation against every wife who gives birth to a child not resembling its father and paternal relations to the same extent it resembles the maternal side. That she has acted treacherously against her husband and the child is a product of adultery! Is there anyone in his right mind who would assume such a depraved connotation to words lightly uttered every day, ideas that don't even enter anyone's thoughts?

If this journalist would accommodate his thinking a bit more, he might understand what any thinking person can understand. That is the impossibility of the Messenger ﷺ remaining silent over such an accusation, rather slander – if this was truly A'isha's intention with her words. He would have certainly spoken out, if not to protect his dignity and honour, he would certainly have done so in keeping to the laws of Allah ﷻ.

Words such as these, if we imagine their meanings to be what this journalist envisages, would require their speaker to be subjected to investigation. And most certainly, the one who should be responsible for this questioning would be Muhammad ﷺ in whose hand was the authority of the state. It would be necessary for him to implement the punishment Allah ﷻ has imposed, upon A'isha ؓ – since she would have accused another of adultery. Then how did the Prophet ﷺ ignore her words and not investigate this accusation, rather this hidden slander by implication? And how did he turn a blind eye to it as if it was a casual joke amongst friends?

But let us return to the words themselves that A'isha ؓ spoke. Where is there the hint of opposition in them, on top of any slanderous accusation?

Hasn't history recorded nothing but Sayidah A'isha's stance of love and dedication to the Messenger ﷺ? To the extent that there remained no place or possibility to conjure up far-fetched meanings to her words about Ibrahim ؑ, which might cause any insult to the Messenger ﷺ?

Wasn't she the one who said to the Messenger ﷺ, when he had asked her permission one night to leave her side to stand and adore his Lord in prayer, 'I love to be by you, but I prefer your wishes'?

Is she not the one who said to him, when he gave her the option to consult her parents on whether to remain with him in marriage, with all the difficulties and abstinence involved, or make her happy with the material means at his disposal and part from her – 'Am I to consult my parents about you, Apostle of

Allah? Rather, I choose Allah and His Messenger and the home of the Hereafter.'

Are these than the words of one who leads an opposing faction against the Messenger of Allah ﷺ? Or was the Prophet's deep love for her because she was this opposing individual deep in the most vulnerable part of his home and family!?

The least a researcher should be equipped with, or aspire to in proposing something from his imagination, is to respect peoples' intelligences and conform to common sense. Whoever belittles minds with his speech and lectures them as if they are fools with techniques of deceit and playing with words, who is blind to common-sense, preferring instead to ramble around its walls, is only imprisoned by his own illusions. And people do not look at him except with the eyes of contempt or pity. No matter how much he refers to schemes against the truth and strives to depose it to crown falsehood in its place, never can he make the truth fall from its station. And falsehood cannot advance to truth's stature no matter what disguise or distortion it resorts to.

A'ISHA IN THE AGE OF THE RIGHTEOUS CALIPHS

Sayidah A'isha's position as a scholar became prominent after the passing of the Messenger of Allah ﷺ as the number of both general and more distinguished enquirers grew, asking for her legal (*fiqhi*) judgements, verification of hadith narrations and consulting her in matters that had confounded them.

As for the Righteous Caliphs ؓ, you would see all of them relying on the consultation of others in difficult matters in which there was no clear textual evidence. And you would see A'isha ؓ at the forefront of those referred to and whose opinion was sought.

During the caliphate of Abu Bakr ؓ, the first successor to the Messenger of Allah ﷺ, some of the wives of the Prophet ﷺ sent Uthman ؓ to remind Abu Bakr ؓ of their inheritances. Someone was sent to consult with Sayidah A'isha ؓ in the matter and she rejected that anything should be bequeathed saying, 'Did not the Messenger of Allah ﷺ say, "We are not inherited from. Whatever we leave behind is to become charity"?'[64]

She also passed through a time of solitude after the passing of the Messenger ﷺ, during which she

---

[64] Bukhari & Muslim

remained in her room by the grave of the Messenger. It was the same period in which Abu Bakr was busy with the wars of apostasy and dealing with those refusing to pay their zakat (alms).

Yet Abu Bakr's rule was short and he passed away after reaching 63 years of age – just like the Prophet – having ruled for just 2 years, 3 months and 10 days.

When Abu Bakr was afflicted with his final sickness, Sayidah A'isha confined herself to care for him. Imam Ahmed narrates in his *Musnad* that when she saw her father on his deathbed, she recited the words of Hatim:

By your life, wealth will not comfort the youth
When the gargle of death tightens the breath.

To which Abu Bakr replied, 'Don't say as such my daughter. But say – **And the agony of death comes with the truth. That is what you were avoiding.**'[65]

She responded with the words of the poet:

His pure face was as if it could seek rain from the clouds
Friend of the orphan and the guardian of the widow.

Abu Bakr replied, 'That, was the Messenger of Allah.'

---

65 Quran; Surah Qaf, (50:19)

Abu Bakr entrusted his will to none other than A'isha, in which he said to A'isha, 'I have conferred to you a garden. But I feel some uneasiness in my soul regarding it. I pray that you return it to the wealth of the Muslims.' And so she did.

He also mentioned in his will, 'As for us, ever since we were given authority over the Muslims, we took not a dinar nor a dirham. We ate from their most unrefined foods and wore their most course of garments on our backs. And we have nothing more or nothing less from the booty of the Muslims than this Abyssinian slave, this mature camel, and this worn-out garment. After I have died, send them to Umar and liberate me from them.'

A'isha implemented his will after his passing, settling all the items of his bequest. When she sent the above-mentioned trusts to Umar, he wept until his tears fell onto the floor and said, 'May Allah have mercy on Abu Bakr. He has set a high example for those who come after him. Allah have mercy on Abu Bakr. He has set a high example for those to come after him.'[66]

Reliance on her knowledge increased in the time of Umar. People would flock to her from far corners to seek her legal judgements (*fatwa*) in difficult religious matters. Umar would refer all difficult matters and issues related to women to her.

---

66 Tabaqaat, Ibn Sa'ad, 3/139

Ibn Sa'ad narrates in *Al-Tabaqaat*, the hadith of Abdul Rahman ibn Qasim from his father, who said, 'A'isha was peerless in giving legal judgements (*fatwa*) during the caliphates of Abu Bakr, Umar, Uthman and until she passed away.'

Umar would show great regard and honour to the Mothers of the Believers, but especially to A'isha. Abeed narrates in his book, *Al-Amwaal*, that when Umar conquered Iraq and Syria and collected the land tax, he gathered the Companions of the Prophet and said, 'I have come of the opinion to allocate this wealth to the families of those who conquered these lands.'

They said, 'An excellent opinion, O Leader of the Believers.'

He asked, 'With whom shall we begin?'

"And who has more right in it than you?' The answered.

He replied, 'No, rather I will begin with the *Ahl ul-Bayt* (family) of the Messenger of Allah. So, he noted down 12,000 for A'isha and 10,000 for each of the other Mothers of the Believers.'

Sayidah A'isha would likewise respect Umar. Ibn Sa'ad narrates that Umar said to his son Abdullah, shortly before his death to rush to the Mother of the Believers, A'isha, and request of her that, 'Umar sends his greetings to you – and do not say Leader of the Believers for I am no leader of the believers today, but say Umar ibn al-Khattab – and he seeks your permission to be buried next to his two companions (i.e. The Prophet ﷺ and Abu Bakr ؓ).'

Abdullah ibn Umar ؓ went forth to seek her permission and she was sitting down, weeping. He greeted her and said, 'Umar sends his greetings of peace upon you and seeks your permission to be buried by his two companions.'

She replied, 'I had wanted that spot for myself, but I prefer it for him this day over myself.'

When he was on his way back, it was mentioned to Umar ؓ that Abdullah had returned. He said, 'Sit me up,' so a man leaned him up against himself, 'What is the response?'

Abdullah ؓ replied, 'As you love, O Leader of the Believers. She has granted you permission to be buried there.'

'Praise is to Allah. There is nothing more important than that resting spot O Abdullah. When I die, carry me upon my crate. Then stop with me at her door. Say Umar ibn Al-Khattab seeks permission to enter. If she grants permission for me, take me through. If she refuses, then take me to the cemetery of the Muslims. For I fear that her permission was because of my position as caliph.'

When he was carried forth, and it was if the Muslims had not been stricken with calamity till that day, Sayidah A'isha ﷺ gave the permission again for him to be buried in that spot that Allah honoured him with, next to his two companions, the Prophet ﷺ and Abu Bakr ﷺ.[67]

Her status only continued to grow during the caliphate of Uthman ibn Affan ﷺ, with even more people coming to seek her legal judgements (*fatwa*) from every distant quarter and city. And Uthman ﷺ showed no less respect and honour to A'isha ﷺ than her predecessor.

Likewise, Sayidah A'isha ﷺ would respect and defend him. In fact, she was independent in narrating may hadiths from the Messenger ﷺ on the virtues of Uthman ﷺ. Amongst which is what Muslim narrates on behalf of A'isha ﷺ that she said, 'The Messenger of Allah ﷺ was laying down in his house with a bit of his leg showing. Abu Bakr ﷺ asked permission to enter and the Prophet ﷺ gave him permission, not stirring or changing his position. Then Umar ﷺ asked permission and the Prophet ﷺ allowed him, still staying in the same state. Then Uthman ﷺ sought permission and the Prophet ﷺ hastened to straighten his garment.' When they left, A'isha ﷺ asked him ﷺ, 'Abu Bakr entered and you did not stir nor rearrange your clothing, then Umar entered and again you

---
67 Sirah Umar ibn Al-Khattab, Ali Tantawi

stirred not. But when Uthman ﷺ entered, you sat up and straightened your garment!?'

The Prophet ﷺ replied, 'Shall I not show modesty to a man to whom even the angels are modest towards?'[68]

Once, she heard some people defaming Uthman ﷺ. She was greatly angered and said, 'May Allah curse whoever curses him. Allah curse whoever curses him. I saw the Messenger of Allah ﷺ while his thigh was touching Uthman ﷺ and I would be wiping the sweat from the brow of the Messenger ﷺ whilst revelation was being descended to him. And the Prophet ﷺ married two of his daughters, one after the other to Uthman. And the Prophet ﷺ would tell him – Write (the revelation), *Uthaym* (little Uthman). Allah ﷻ would not put a slave in such an intimate position with his Messenger ﷺ, except if that slave was beloved to Him.'[69]

And she was the one who narrated from the Messenger ﷺ that he said to Uthman, 'O Uthman, perhaps Allah will clothe you with a mantle, if they want to remove it from you, take it not off for them.'[70]

Sayidah A'isha ﷺ remained upon her goodwill and respect to Uthman ﷺ until he was assassinated. She was then amongst the first who demanded justice against his killers.

---

68 Sahih Muslim, Fadhail Uthman
69 Sayidah A'isha, Abdul Hameed Tahmaz.
70 Tirmidhi

Some modern-day writes have claimed that this goodwill was also intermixed with disagreements and that A'isha ﷺ bore a grudge because some of his stances and actions. Some even accuse her of playing a part in stirring the people up against Uthman ﷺ, until the matter ended so devastatingly.

What is regrettable is that those who make such false claims rely on the book, *Al-Aghani* and *Al-Aqd Al-Fareed* by Ibn Abd Rabihi and others like them. What both the masses and scholars well know, is that these authors gathered scattered reports in their books, like a lumberjack who goes to work at night and knows not what he has gathered on his back, they have not differentiated between the authentic, weak, or even fabricated narrations. Their interest was only in exciting the reader with dramatic and rare reports, whatever its source or however low its credibility and value.

But it is not the place, in this small book, to repeat such writers' claims and expose the falsehood in their books and conceptions. Let us refer to a detailed work that deals with the matter comprehensively. Penned by Professor Abdul Hameed Tahmaaz, you may consult *Al-Sayidah A'isha, Umm al Mumineen wa A'limah Nisa' Al-Islam* (As-Sayidah A'isha, Mother of the Believers and Scholar of the Women of Islam).

But perhaps in Sayidah A'isha's previously mentioned words, when she said in anger, 'May Allah curse whoever curses Uthman. Allah curse whoever curses Uthman...', is what dismantles every nonsensical argument that would have us envisage that A'isha ﷺ was spiteful to Uthman ﷺ or that she had a part to play in inciting the people against him.

Unfortunately, there are people today who also confuse the matter of legal (*ijtihadi*) differences, which the Companions ﷺ were well known to have and personal disputes built upon grudge and spite. The latter is a baseness far below the nobility of the Companions ﷺ, A'isha ﷺ foremost amongst them.

Certainly, Sayidah A'isha ﷺ did differ from the other Companions ﷺ in some legal (*fiqhi*) opinions and even in theological and social matters. Zarkashi has gathered some points of difference in his work (*Al-Ijabah fi mah Istadrakathu A'isha Ala Sahabah*). She also differed with Uthman ﷺ on some of his political judgements, some of which she referred to in her discussion with Imran ibn Haseen (as previously mentioned).

But these disagreements entailed no grudge like some would like to imagine. If it were true, why would she stand up against the killers of Uthman ﷺ and set out against them in uproar, seeking justice and vengeance for him? The calamity of these writers is that they compare the Companions of the Messenger of Allah ﷺ to themselves.

They only employ their opinions to further fuel their agendas and dogmatism, they see their adopted opinions as the ultimate religion of their truth, besides which no other faith exists. And so, they discredit and mislead the followers of different methodologies, understandings, and opinions, whatever they may be. They see it only right to ignite feelings of hostility because of their convictions. According to them, the disagreements between the Companions ؉ should be judged by the scales of their own differences, division and hostility. And if Sayidah A'isha ؉ held a political opinion different to what Uthman ؉ followed, well that fits nicely into their narrative of resentment and opposition and is in concordance with their animosity of today. But their forging as so is even worse than resentment or hostility. Indeed, the greater crime is perpetrated in propping up this false scale of justice.

If you find it difficult to understand the painful events that followed, that is, the fighting between the Companions ؉, you may peruse the contents of the next chapter.

***

When Uthman ؉ was killed, A'isha ؉ was at the forefront of those calling for allegiance to be given to Ali ؉. None asked her about who was most deserving of the leadership of the Muslims after Uthman ؉, except that she insisted on Ali ؉ and that allegiance be given to him.

Al Hafiz ibn Hajar ؉ narrates from Tabari from Ahnaf ibn Qais who said, 'After we performed the Hajj, people had gathered in the middle of the Prophet's Masjid. I met with Talha ﷺ and Zubayr ﷺ and said, "I don't see Uthman except that he will be killed. To whom shall I ally myself after him?"

They replied, 'Ali'.

I then travelled to Mecca and called upon A'isha ﷺ and the news of the killing of Uthman ﷺ had reached us. I asked her, "Who do you order me to ally myself to?"

She replied, "Ali".

So, I returned back to Medina and pledged my allegiance to Ali ﷺ before heading back to Basrah.'[71]

A'isha ﷺ would also hold Ali ﷺ in high esteem and would on occasion praise him for his great knowledge. She would refer many of those with questions to him, making known his virtue, status, and closeness with the Messenger of Allah ﷺ.

And nothing distorts the image of mutual respect and honour between Ali ﷺ and A'isha ﷺ upon some researchers, except her concern for revenge against the killers of Uthman ﷺ, her striving of justice for him, her march to Basra and the heated war and confusion of the Battle of Jamal.

Once you realise that amongst researchers and

---

[71] Fath al-Bari 13/27

writers are those who have made a career of spinning lies against the alive and the dead, to confuse clear historical events so to befuddle an unsuspecting audience, you will realise the difficulty in penetrating these veils of schemes and plots to arrive at the true picture and reality of these historical events.

Yet whatever the case, any researcher who truthfully want to pass beyond these confusions to reach clear reality, free from additions and forgeries, will certainly find his way open for that.

THE BATTLE OF AL-JAMAL, A DARK TRIBULATION

Let us now turn with a few words, appropriate to this brief book, to uncover the true nature of this tragedy and the hidden hands that ignited the fuel to blaze an inferno. Let us pass over small, side events that clutter the matter and over too, the egos of writers inspired by their diverse imaginations. Let us also keep bereft from analysing history through one's personal opinions – a methodology that has always made history testify to what it never witnessed and shaded it with fantasies it is both free and far from.

During the turbulence at the end of Uthman's rule, the wives of the Prophet had left for Hajj that year to flee from the tribulation that was occurring in the capital of Medina. The news of Uthman's murder reached them there and they decided to remain in Mecca, until the reality of the situation became apparent.

During this period, the pledge of allegiance was completed to our master, Ali in Medina. Zubair and Talha had pledged allegiance to him and after they had roused others to do so too, they asked permission to perform Umrah and so were now also present in Mecca. That year, Ya'la ibn Umayyah was also present in Mecca, who was the governor of Uthman over Yemen. A large number of the leading Companions and the Mothers of the Believers were hence gathered and they took counsel amongst themselves regarding the assassination and the proper course of action.

Sayidah A'isha ﷺ addressed them, calling for the price of Uthman's blood. The leader of the believers, Ali ﷺ, had already affirmed to the Companions ﷺ the need to seek justice from his murderers but he had asked for time so that the disarray in the state could first settle and so that he could also deal with the revolt of the people of Sham under the leadership of Muawiya ﷺ. But the people were moved to answer the call of A'isha ﷺ and pronounced that they would march forward for justice for Uthman ﷺ as long as she marched on with them.

The discussion then turned to where they should first set out. Sham, Medina and Basra were all mentioned until they finally settled on Basra in Iraq. When they headed off, and they were a few thousand, they passed one night by watering spot called *Al-Hawab*. At their passing, the dogs of *Al-Hawab* began barking. A'isha ﷺ asked, 'What is the name of this place?'

They replied, 'It is *Al-Hawab*.'

She hit one hand over the other and said, 'To Allah we belong and to Him do we return! We must go back!'

They said, 'Why so?'

She said, 'I heard the Messenger of Allah saying to his wives, "I wish I would know which of you it is, to whom the dogs of *Al-Hawab* will bark at."'

She then stopped her camel and made it kneel and said, 'Take me back! Take me back! By Allah I am the one of *Al-Hawab*!'[72]

Then her nephew, Abdullah ibn Zubayr, came and said, 'The one who has informed you that this is the water of Al-Hawab has lied.' And he continued until he had convinced her to resume the journey to Basra.

When they reached the gates of Basra, Uthman bin Haneef, the governor Uthman had appointed over Basra, questioned them on the intentions of their arrival. A'isha replied, 'We have come to demand the price for the blood of Uthman.'

Uthman ibn Haneef discussed the matter with his advisers. One said, 'If they came for the blood of Uthman, then we are not his killers. Send them back from whence they came.' Another said, 'They only came to seek our aid against the killers of Uthman, who are amongst us and elsewhere.' And Uthman ibn Haneef knew from circulating talk that the killers of Uthman had helpers in Basra.

Sayidah A'isha and those with her camped

---

72 Ibn Kathir narrates this hadith as amongst the evidence of Prophethood. Al-Bidayah wa Al-Nihaya, Ibn Kathir, 7/232

on the outskirts of the city in a place called *Mirbad*. Those that wanted to join her camp, left Basra to do so. And she continued to encourage people to the necessity of seeking justice for Uthman ﷺ.

During this period, Hakeem ibn Jablah, who was allied with the group that killed Uthman ﷺ, gathered his allies and launched an attack on A'isha's camp. And initially, the camp of the Mother of the Believers held back from engaging them.

But Hakeem persisted and broke through their lines with his men and fighting ensued with nothing stopping it except the coming of night. Fighting continued the second day, with many dying from the side of Hakeem ibn Jublah. The army of A'isha ﷺ, Talhah ﷺ and Zubayr ﷺ had nearly occupied the entire city, the city's treasury already in their grasp. The killers were down to about 300 men led by Hakeem bin Jublah. The army of A'isha ﷺ made a final, devastating assault forward with the result that Hakeem and no less than 70 of his men, were finally killed.

As for Ali, may Allah be well-pleased with him, he changed his march from Sham to head for Basra when he heard about what had ensued. He was asked, 'O Commander of the Believers, what do you intend by leading us to Basra?'

Ali ﷺ replied, 'What we intend is peace (with the army of A'isha) if they accept it and respond to it.'

'And if they don't respond?'

'We will ignore their violation of our sovereignty, give them their rights and show patience.'

'And if they aren't satisfied?'

'We will leave them alone as long as they leave us alone.'

'And if they don't leave us alone?'

'We will refrain ourselves from them.'

The man replied, 'Then yes, let us march forth.'

On the way to Kufa, a man came from it by the name of Amir ibn Matr Al-Shaybani. Ali ﷺ asked him what news he had with him and he informed Ali ﷺ about all that had transpired in Basra. Ali ﷺ then asked about Abu Musa Al-Ashari ﷺ.

To which Amir replied, 'If you want peace, then Abu Musa is your man. If you desire war, then he is not.'

Ali ﷺ replied, 'By Allah, I do not want except peace.'

Then Ali ﷺ sent a messenger to Abu Musa Al-Ashari ﷺ, the governor of Uthman over Kufa and envoys were exchanged between them. Among the envoys from Ali's side were Ammar ibn Yasir ﷺ and Al-Hassan ﷺ, the son of Ali ﷺ. During these delegations, Ammar ﷺ heard someone curse A'isha ﷺ and he replied to him, 'Be silent with your mad barking. By Allah, she is the wife of the Messenger in this world and the next. But Allah is testing you with her to see if you obey Him or her.'[73]

Ammar ﷺ and Al-Hassan ﷺ called the people in Kufa to go and seek peace and unity with the Commander of the Believers, Ali ﷺ. The people responded and close to 12,000 men left with them to see Ali ﷺ and he received them and said, 'O people of Kufa, who met the kings of non-Arabs and defeated them. I have called you to witness our brethren in Basra. If they return, then that is what we seek. If they reject, we shall treat them with kindness up until they treat us with oppression. And we would never leave a matter except that we have preferred peace and reconciliation over corruption, if Allah wills.'

Then Ali ﷺ dispatched Al-Qa'qa' ibn Amr ﷺ, who newly joined him in Kufa, as a messenger to the camp of Sayidah A'isha ﷺ at Basra to call them to unity and harmony with the Commander of the Believers. Al-Qa'qa' ﷺ first went to visit the Mother of the Believers and said, 'O mother…what has brought you to these lands?'

She replied, 'My son, it is to redress the wrongs amongst the people.'

---
[73] Bukhari

He requested from her if she could send for Talha ﷺ and Zubair ﷺ so they too may be present. Al-Qa'qa' ﷺ said to them, 'I asked the Mother of the Believers what has brought her here and she said it is to redress the wrongs between the people.'

They replied, 'And the same has brought us.'

Al-Qa'qa' ﷺ continued, 'Then inform me what is the nature of this redressing and for what reason is it?'

They replied, 'It is against the murderers of Uthman, if this matter is neglected, then that is neglecting the Qur'an.'

He replied, 'You two have killed the plotters from the people of Basra. But you were, before you had slayed them, closer to righteousness than you are today. You killed perhaps 600 men, on whose account 6000 others have been angered and disassociated from you. To the extent that you demanded Harqoos ibn Zuhair and 6000 men prevented you from him. If you are now to let them free, then you would have contradicted yourselves. And if you continue to fight, you will cause even greater division than what you are trying to remedy. And just as you are incapable to avenge Uthman ﷺ by taking Harqoos ibn Zuhair because of 6000 men standing in your way, Ali ﷺ is more excused in deferring justice against the killers of Uthman ﷺ. He only delays punishing them until it is feasible for him to do so.'

Sayidah A'isha ﷺ asked, 'And what do you suggest?'

He replied, 'I say let the matter settle first, for once it has settled, they will disintegrate. If you come to terms with us, it is a sign of goodness and mercy to come, as well as a step towards attaining justice for Uthman ﷺ. But if you reject us out of stubbornness, it will be an evil precedent that will lead to the downfall of this sovereignty of ours.'

They said, 'You have spoken the truth. If Ali ﷺ comes with the same opinion as you, then the matter will be reconciled.'

Al-Qa'qa ﷺ returned and informed Ali ﷺ, who was much gladdened by their response and he ensured his party also be inclined to peace. Sayidah A'isha ﷺ also sent him a letter affirming she had only come to remedy wrongs and uphold justice and both parties were content. Ali ﷺ spoke with the people and informed them of this understanding and they set out to Basra the next day to join with the army of A'isha ﷺ.

A'isha ﷺ, Talha ﷺ and Zubair ﷺ also went forward to receive him. Some suggested to Talha ﷺ and Zubair ﷺ to take this opportunity to attack those who they knew to be from the killers of Uthman ﷺ. But they replied, 'The Commander of the Believers has asked that this whole matter be pacified first and we have delegated the matter to him.'

And then there were those who questioned Ali ﷺ while he was headed for Basra, 'Do they have any basis for the blood they are asking (against Uthman's killers)?'

He replied, 'Yes.'

'And do you have any basis for delaying this justice?'

'Yes.'

'Then what is to become of us tomorrow if we are tested (with war)?'

'I hope that none from either us or them is killed whose heart Allah ﷻ has purified, except that He enters them into Paradise.'

The two parties advanced, with hearts reassured and minds at ease and with the consensus that the matter will be deferred to Ali, the Commander of the Believers. He would be the one to solve it at the appropriate time. The people spent – as Ibn Kathir says – their best night. As for the killers of Uthman, they spent their worst.

But then what happened that the matter ended so dreadfully?

It was a chain of plots, one after the other, that in fact began with the killing of Uthman ﷺ. It was directed towards ripping apart the unity of the Muslims and bringing about cracks and splinters in their young civilisation. The men behind these intrigues were strangers to the body of Islam as represented by these two parties of Ali ﷺ and A'isha ﷺ.

So, when the two armies met, united in purpose, these schemers were also present. They have been named as primarily Al-Ashfar Al-Nakhai, Shareeh ibn Awfa, Abdullah ibn Saba' also commonly known as Ibn Sawda, Salim ibn Thalabah, and Ghulam ibn Al-Haytham. And there was none among them, praise be to Allah, who could claim to be a companion of the Messenger ﷺ, as Ibn Kathir mentions. The worst of them and foremost in evil schemes was Abdullah ibn Saba.[74] Thousands of men were gathered behind them. They deliberated amongst themselves of the danger upon them if the group of Ali ﷺ and that of A'isha ﷺ would band together. They realised that their reconciliation would be the harbinger of peril for them. One even audaciously stated, 'Then we will

---

74 See his biography in the books of history and biographies. Amongst which is Al-Bida wa Al-Tarikh 5/129, Lisaan Al-Mizaan 3/289, Tahdheeb ibn Asaakir 7/428, Mizaan Al-Ia'tidaal 2/426, Al-Bidaya wa Al-Nihaya in various locations such as 7/240. All his biographies relate that he was a fanatical heretic. Al-Dhahabi mentions of him: He was himself astray and would lead others astray. He would claim that the Qur'an was only one of nine parts and only Ali knew of the other parts. It is thought that Ali burned him to death.
Strange it is that among Shiites today, some stubbornly insist that he is an imaginary figure...but then why are the rest of the historians and biographers in consensus about his existence, from the time of the Tabieen (generation immediately following the Companions) until our day today? Is he now suddenly an imaginary figure after 14 centuries!?

follow Uthman with Ali!'

But Abdullah ibn Saba scoffed at that idea and advised them, 'Your salvation is in infiltrating the people. When they come together, incite war between them and don't let them unite. Defend yourselves by impelling those around you to war.'

They dispersed after agreeing to his opinion and instructed their people to also enact this plot. They were to slip into the rows of men in the dark of night and provoke a war, each to those around him, whatever the cost.

Then think about this strife when it reared its many actors, in the depth of night, how understandable it is that they made the Muslims lose their sound judgement and firm footing. How they were robbed of their opportunity to deliberate and show prudence. And how they could not but be drawn into that hurricane surrounding them.

Ibn Kathir ﷺ, who is among the most trustworthy in the relating of these events with objectivity and insight relates:

'So those schemers, around 2000 of them, arose before the onset of Fajr. And each man amongst them threw himself with swords at those in whose camp he was embedded. Both Muslim camps roused their people to defend themselves, stirring from their sleep to their weapons. On one side they said – the people of Kufa have struck us while we slept at night, double crossing us –

136 - THE BATTLE OF AL-JAMAL, A DARK TRIBULATION

thinking it was a clear ploy from the party of Ali ﷺ.

On the other side, when the commotion reached Ali ﷺ, he asked, "What is it with the people?"

"While we slept, we were laid upon and betrayed by the people of Basra!"

And each rushed to his weapon, donned his armour, and mounted his horse. None was the wiser to what had truly occurred. It was the decree of Allah, coming to pass.

Battle ensued between the two Muslim parties. With Ali ﷺ there were 20,000 men, while with A'isha ﷺ, 30,000 – and certainly to Allah we belong and to Him we shall return. And the people of Ibn Sabah lost no energy in shedding blood, while Ali's caller was shouting out to one and all, "Will you not stop!? Will you not stop!?" But there was none to hearken to his words.'[75]

I don't see any goodness to come of discussing this matter further, after we have been acquainted with what flowed of tribulation and schemes up to this point. This trial, which robbed all men of their wills, let no one deliberate, nor unite or to hold their ranks.

And how I wish we could see our own states, if one of us was startled awake in middle of the night, finding himself in the midst of such turmoil, knowing neither its cause nor where to escape to! Is there anything for him to do, but defend himself from

---
75 Al Bidaya wa Al Nihaya, Ibn Kathir. 7/240

this surprise attack? Does he defend himself with anything other than the same weapons he is being attacked with?

This then is how this tribulation churned over thousands of innocents from both sides by way of this despicable and cunning plot, which was not realised except after the fact. And the followers of Ibn Sabah had surrounded the howdah of Sayidah A'isha ؓ and began altogether striking it with a volley of arrows. She called out, 'My sons…(remember) Allah! Recall the Day of Account!' Yet they continued to shoot at her howdah, until it looked like the back of a porcupine.

The army of Ali ؓ moved forward to protect her howdah and surrounded it with extraordinary courage and began guiding it through the ranks until it reached Ali's ؓ position. The war itself was going back and forth and large numbers of men were killed. And the hands of seventy men were cut as they tried to take the reins of the camel of A'isha ؓ.

Some members from the army of Ali ؓ observed that men will continue to attack the howdah as long as its camel remained standing. It is said Al-Qa'qa' ؓ gave the order that the camel be hamstrung so that Sayidah A'isha ؓ would no longer be a target. Once the camel fell, those attacking it were routed. The howdah was then carried away to a place distant from the arena of death and war.

How quickly after that did Ali ؓ rush to her,

greeting her and enquiring of her safety. He asked, 'How are you, O Mother?' When she replied that she was well, Ali ﷺ said, 'May Allah forgive you.' Then the Companions ﷺ came, one after the other, from every direction, sending their greetings upon her and resting their minds that she was safe.

***

After narrating these facts, which no historian of noble intentions and sound heart can deny, I could continue describing the scenes of this tragedy, details of different reports, and what the fierce winds of this calamity provoked like many writers of today.

But what goodness could be hoped to come of that? Or what hidden truth uncovered and attained through such scavenging? Other than the painful truths we have already realised and which, no fair-minded researcher doubts.

It is the pinnacle of wonder, that you find writers of this event today, causing division amongst those two Muslim groups, with the teeth of their pens and with slander and criticism. When nothing motivated the Muslims except the upholding of Islam and nothing provoked them, except the rules of the Shariah. Such were the sentiments of Sayidah A'isha ﷺ, Talha ﷺ and Zubair ﷺ. Then these writers direct no remark, not even a sidenote, to those heads of this tribulation who schemed by night, like Ibn Saba.

You have seen what he proposed to his companions when receiving the news of the two Muslim groups uniting and their deference of the matter to Ali ﷺ. How they proposed to slip into the lines of sincere, concurring brothers and incite unexpected storms of confusion to set one upon the other.

How strange that these writers add even more victims to this misfortune, by attacking, vilifying, criticising, and accusing. Then they don't draw any attention to the craftsmen of it, the over-seers of it and blowers of its fire from the killing of Uthman ﷺ and ending with the killing of Ali, may Allah ennoble his blessed face.

They write long pages about these confrontations that the Muslims were compelled to, they feign concern over the unity that was split and over its Muslim victims. Yet this supposed sentiment did not encourage them to utter a single word censuring – and I don't go as far to say discrediting or condemning – those who harassed that unity with their scheming, shed with their swords that blood and infiltrated in the death of darkness so that many an innocent one would sink their sword in the neck of another innocent one so that war might decimate them all.

Is it not right for any thinker to be certain that this absorption in attacking those innocent ones, without turning an eyelid to those who concocted this tribulation and persisted in it, is just the latest episode of the very same plot? And if not, are such writers anything other than cross-eyed, squinting through the darkness to then descend with an attack upon the oppressed?

A'ISHA DURING THE RULE OF MUAWIYA

Sayidah A'isha ﷺ returned to Medina from that distant arena that witnessed the spilling of blood of innocents, as but a mass of pain, regret and grief. She had left to mend the rift between the Muslims, restore the peace and put an end to the tribulation that was born with the killing Uthman ﷺ. But returned with the rift being widened, the peace deteriorated, and the tribulation ignited, now raging like a beast broken free from its reigns.

Regret started eating up her heart, grief was melting her, and her tears did not cease flowing over the part she played in causing blood to be shed, without any benefit achieved or sign that the tribulations were being suppressed.

They say when she was sitting, reciting the Qur'an and passed by His Words, '**And stay in your homes...**'[76], a crying like wailing would overwhelm her. And she would repeat it, blaming herself over the stance she so daringly took.

She isolated herself now, may the Good-Pleasure of Allah be upon her, from everything. Keeping only to her worship, Qur'an, charity, devoutness, and answering to the questions of the people, who would continue to arrive for knowledge

---
76 Quran, Surah Ahzab, (33:33).

and legal judgements (*fatwa*).

During this period, Muawiya ﷺ tried to gain her support, however she was not the least bit interested, especially since the matter had become more turbid due to him, or at the hands of his followers.

Among the more prominent of these turmoils, was the killing of her brother, Muhammad ibn Abi Bakr ﷺ, whom Ali ﷺ had placed as governor over Egypt. Muawiya's men had roused against him after Muawiya ﷺ supplied them with a large army. Muhammad ibn Abi Bakr was captured and then put to death. A'isha ﷺ was greatly grieved by his killing and gathered his family and children to take care of them and show compassion towards them.

Another was the matter of Marwan ibn Al-Hakam, who was the governor over Medina before Muawiya came to power. Marwan had prevented Al-Hassan ﷺ, son of Ali ﷺ, to be buried in the honoured chamber of the Messenger ﷺ, even after A'isha ﷺ had given permission for it. Al-Hussein, may Allah's Good-Pleasure be upon him, had insisted his brother be buried by his grandfather, the Prophet ﷺ. The matter was about to implode into another tribulation, if not for some of the Companions advising him and persuading him to submit to the order of Marwan. Al-Hassan ﷺ was eventually buried close to his blessed mother, Fatimah ﷺ in Jannatul Baqi.

Whatever Muawiya ﷺ would send Sayidah

A'isha ﷺ, and he sent her large amounts of wealth, nothing of that would remain with her. She would hastily distribute it among the poor, as we previously mentioned.

Muawiya ﷺ would follow the way of the caliphs before him too, in consulting her and seeking guidance through her opinion. It is reported that he once wrote to her seeking some advice in concise words. To which she wrote back:

'Peace be upon you.
Indeed, I have heard the Messenger of Allah ﷺ saying, "Whoever seeks the Good-pleasure of Allah ﷺ by displeasing the people, then Allah ﷺ will free him from dependence upon the people. And whoever seeks the pleasure of people by displeasing Allah ﷺ, Allah ﷺ will entrust his affair to the people."
And peace be upon you.'

It has also been soundly narrated that A'isha ﷺ would disapprove of many of Muawiya's actions. Perhaps the most strongly of which she renounced, was his killing of Hijr ibn Uday and his companions, who were wrongly accused and slandered.

Al-Tabari narrated that when Muawiya ﷺ was performing the Hajj, he passed by the house of A'isha ﷺ and asked permission to visit A'isha. He was allowed entry and when he had sat down she asked him, 'Are you in such sound mind, that I have not concealed someone to attack you?'

He replied, 'I have entered a house of peace.'

'O Muawiya, then are you not in fear of Allah ﷻ over your killing of Hijr and his companions?'

He replied, 'It wasn't I who killed them, but those that testified against them.'[77]

Al-Tabari then mentions another narration from Ibn Sireen that A'isha said, 'O Muawiya, where was your insight regarding Hijr?'

He replied, 'O Mother of the Believers, clear thinking was absent from me.'

Ibn Sireen continues, 'It has reached us that on his deathbed, Muawiya was saying, "I have a long day in front of me because of you, O Hijr! A long day indeed..."'

---

[77] Tabari, 5/259.

HER LAST DAYS & DEATH

Sayidah A'isha ﷺ continued to grow in devotion, worship, asceticism and isolation from the people, except to receive them to convey knowledge, giving fatwa and clarifying the halal and haram.

She was frequent in her supererogatory prayers at night and day and persisted in performing the five daily prayers in congregation. She would either be following the imam of the masjid from her house – it being connected to the masjid – or she would gather a group of women and lead them.

When she became sick with the illness that would claim her life, in Ramadan, the 58th year after the Hijra, she advised that her funeral procession not be followed by torch fire, nor any fancy cloth used on her crate.

When her sickness worsened, Abdullah ibn Abbas ﷺ requested permission to visit her. Ibn Kathir narrates from Dhikwan, the doorman of the house of A'isha, that 'Abdullah ibn Abbas came seeking permission to visit A'isha while I was present. With her was her nephew, Abdullah ibn Abdul Rahman. I said Ibn Abbas has come seeking permission and she was amid her last breaths.

She said, "Let me be alone from Ibn Abbas.'

He said, "O mother, indeed Ibn Abbas is from your righteous children, he sends his greetings on you and to bid you farewell."

She replied, "Grant him permission if you so want." And I allowed him to enter.

When he had sat down, he said, 'Glad tidings to you.'

She asked, 'For what?'

"Nothing separates you from meeting Muhammad ﷺ and your beloved ones, except the soul leaving the body. You were the most beloved of his wives to him. And the Messenger ﷺ would not love except the good and pure. And it was when your necklace had fallen on the night of *Al-Abwa* and the Messenger ﷺ and his Companions had no water left, that Allah sent down the verses of *tayammum*. And it was because of you that Allah revealed that concession to this nation. And Allah revealed your innocence from above seven heavens, and that too through the Trustworthy Spirit (Angel Jibril), so that there is not a masjid of Allah except that it (i.e., your innocence and purity) is recited in it, during the night and the day."

She replied, "Let me be O ibn Abbas. By the One in whose hand is my soul, if only I was a thing forgotten and abandoned...'[78]

---

[78] Al Bidaya wa Al Nihaya, 8/94.

Ibn Kathir prefers the opinion that she passed away on the night of Tuesday, 17th of Ramadan. She requested that she be buried in Jannatul Baqi at night. Abu Huraira ﷺ lead her funeral prayer after the witr prayer. Five people lowered her down into her grave, amongst them was her nephews, Abdullah and Urwa, sons of her sister Asma bint Abi Bakr ﷺ and Zubair ﷺ.

She had arrived at the age of 67 years – if she was 18 when the Messenger of Allah ﷺ passed away and 9 years old at the first year of hijra. And Allah's Good-Pleasure and Mercy be upon her eternally.

HER MOST FAMOUS STUDENTS

Several students of knowledge distinguished themselves at the hands of Sayidah A'isha ﷺ. And they were from amongst the most knowledgeable and famous of the *tabieen*. They would sit as students behind a curtain while Sayidah A'isha ﷺ taught them from the other side.

Some of these students were close relatives to A'isha ﷺ and she would especially concern herself with their education. Because of their close family ties with her, they had greater opportunity to sit and learn from her. From them was Abdullah ibn Zubair and Urwa ibn Zubair – sons of her sister Asma, Al-Qasim ibn Muhammad – her nephew from her brother, Abdullah ibn Abi Ateeq – the grandson of her brother, Ibaad and Khubayb – the sons of her nephew, Abdullah ibn Zubair, Ibad ibn Hamza ibn Abdullah ibn Zubayr and Abu Salamah ibn Abdul Rahman – son of her sister from rid a'a (breastfeeding).[79]

Urwa was perhaps the one who benefitted most from her knowledge and narrated from her the most. He was amongst the most brilliant scholars of Medina, was born near the end of the caliphate of Umar ibn al-Khattab ﷺ and his age at the battle of al-

---

[79] As Sayidah A'isha, Abdul Al-Hameed Tahmaaz, pg 201.

Jamal was 13 years old.

Qabisha ibn Dhib mentions, 'Urwa gained ascendancy over us by his sitting with A'isha. He was the most knowledgeable of people with the hadiths of A'isha. He was an authority in a great number of hadiths. He was a scholar, faqih, trustworthy and reliable.'

AFTERWORD

Dear reader,

This then is a dense, and I believe inclusive, summary of the biography of the Mother of the Believers, A'isha ﷺ. I have relied on the soundest sources and drawn from the most truthful of tongues – far from the influences of fanaticism and heedlessness of whims.

You have seen in what we have recounted, of her elevated morals, pure upbringing, her noble descent and lineage, the vastness of her knowledge, truthfulness of her devoutness, plenitude of her worship, intensity of her asceticism and righteousness, her veneration and esteem for the rest of the Companions ﷺ, especially to his pure family – at their forefront Ali ﷺ. You have seen in what we have recounted in all that, what reveals the secret of the Prophet's love for her and her capturing of his heart, like no other of his blessed wives.

And if she had none of these virtues and excellences except for this strength of love from the Messenger ﷺ, which only grew as their days spent together increased, until he left this world in her embrace – then that is sufficient a testament to her merit. One that all the righteous slaves of Allah ﷻ and his pure angels can attest to. Then ponder at her merit, with all her virtues considered with the love of the Messenger ﷺ sitting as a crown on top of her head.

She was one who refused to let herself or the Muslims turn a blind eye to the murder of Uthman ؓ and demanded justice for him. She was pushed to this cause for a motive none disputed with in its essence – foremost Ali ؓ.

However, she did not know, nor did anyone from the noble Companions, that the heads of this tribulation had established, in the darkness of night, a snare to fetter them by. If it was not for this plot, the consequence of those movements would have achieved justice, solidarity, and strength for the Muslims. And the Islamic brotherhood would have been purified from contaminants.

If the fruit of that venture was paradise, like they appeared to her and how she judged the matter, then she entered it, praise be to Allah ﷻ. And if it was hellfire, as they appeared afterwards, then she left that arena hastily, never to return, under the Protection of Allah ﷻ and His Kindness.

Can you not then doubt, dear reader, that all written about her built upon imaginations sourced from gutters flowing from the swamp of spiteful hypocrisy which burst forth from the person of Abdullah ibn Ubay, or depending on dark plots that continue until this day from the dark mind of Ibn Saba

– can you then not doubt that it is departing from the truth, favouring falsehood, two things that there is clear difference and distinction between? That it is turning away from pure, abundant springs to favour the dry dregs of tribalism and whims?

And I bear witness that anyone who turns a blind eye to all these facts, that have been established by trustworthy and sound biographers and writers and then turns his heart into a container of spite and hatred against Sayidah A'isha ﷺ – that he possesses a decayed heart and extends his animosity towards her loving husband, who insisted on dying in her lap, Muhammad, the Messenger of Allah ﷺ. Such a person does not even perceive the significance and implications of their hatred towards Sayidah A'isha ﷺ.

I ask Allah ﷺ, that he purifies our hearts from impurities and that He make from our love to the Messenger of Allah ﷺ his family, including his wives, and his faithful, noble Companions, a capital that we accumulate for our success on the Day that people shall stand before the Lord of the Worlds. If our righteous deeds are lacking on the scales of goodness, and the weight of our negligence and disobediences exceed it, may He magnify our love for them as a deliverer and eloquent intercessor, and praise be to Allah ﷺ, Lord of the Worlds.

- Dr Muhammad Saeed Ramadan Al-Bouti ﷺ.

www.ingramcontent.com/pod-product-compliance
Lightning Source LLC
Chambersburg PA
CBHW022016290426
44109CB00015B/1196